AI
Self-Driving Cars
Equanimity

Practical Advances in
Artificial Intelligence and Machine Learning

Dr. Lance B. Eliot, MBA, PhD

DEDICATION

To my incredible daughter, Lauren, and my incredible son, Michael.

Forest fortuna adiuvat (from the Latin; good fortune favors the brave).

CONTENTS

Dr. Lance B. Eliot

ACKNOWLEDGMENTS

I have been the beneficiary of advice and counsel by many friends, colleagues, family, investors, and many others. I want to thank everyone that has aided me throughout my career. I write from the heart and the head, having experienced first-hand what it means to have others around you that support you during the good times and the tough times.

To Warren Bennis, one of my doctoral advisors and ultimately a colleague, I offer my deepest thanks and appreciation, especially for his calm and insightful wisdom and support.

To Mark Stevens and his generous efforts toward funding and supporting the USC Stevens Center for Innovation.

To Lloyd Greif and the USC Lloyd Greif Center for Entrepreneurial Studies for their ongoing encouragement of founders and entrepreneurs.

To Peter Drucker, William Wang, Aaron Levie, Peter Kim, Jon Kraft, Cindy Crawford, Jenny Ming, Steve Milligan, Chis Underwood, Frank Gehry, Buzz Aldrin, Steve Forbes, Bill Thompson, Dave Dillon, Alan Fuerstman, Larry Ellison, Jim Sinegal, John Sperling, Mark Stevenson, Anand Nallathambi, Thomas Barrack, Jr., and many other innovators and leaders that I have met and gained mightily from doing so.

Thanks to Ed Trainor, Kevin Anderson, James Hickey, Wendell Jones, Ken Harris, DuWayne Peterson, Mike Brown, Jim Thornton, Abhi Beniwal, Al Biland, John Nomura, Eliot Weinman, John Desmond, and many others for their unwavering support during my career.

And most of all thanks as always to Lauren and Michael, for their ongoing support and for having seen me writing and heard much of this material during the many months involved in writing it. To their patience and willingness to listen.

Dr. Lance B. Eliot

INTRODUCTION

This is a book that provides the newest innovations and the latest Artificial Intelligence (AI) advances about the emerging nature of AI-based autonomous self-driving driverless cars. Via recent advances in Artificial Intelligence (AI) and Machine Learning (ML), we are nearing the day when vehicles can control themselves and will not require and nor rely upon human intervention to perform their driving tasks (or, that <u>allow</u> for human intervention, but only *require* human intervention in very limited ways).

Similar to my other related books, which I describe in a moment and list the chapters in the Appendix A of this book, I am particularly focused on those advances that pertain to self-driving cars. The phrase "autonomous vehicles" is often used to refer to any kind of vehicle, whether it is ground-based or in the air or sea, and whether it is a cargo hauling trailer truck or a conventional passenger car. Though the aspects described in this book are certainly applicable to all kinds of autonomous vehicles, I am focused more so here on cars.

Indeed, I am especially known for my role in aiding the advancement of self-driving cars, serving currently as the Executive Director of the Cybernetic AI Self-Driving Cars Institute. In addition to writing software, designing and developing systems and software for self-driving cars, I also speak and write quite a bit about the topic. This book is a collection of some of my more advanced essays. For those of you that might have seen my essays posted elsewhere, I have updated them and integrated them into this book as one handy cohesive package.

You might be interested in companion books that I have written that provide additional key innovations and fundamentals about self-driving cars. Those books are entitled **"Introduction to Driverless Self-Driving Cars," "Advances in AI and Autonomous Vehicles: Cybernetic Self-Driving Cars," "Self-Driving Cars: "The Mother of All AI Projects," "Innovation and Thought Leadership on Self-Driving Driverless Cars," "New Advances in AI Autonomous Driverless Self-Driving Cars," "Autonomous Vehicle Driverless Self-Driving Cars and Artificial Intelligence," "Transformative Artificial Intelligence Driverless Self-Driving Cars," "Disruptive Artificial Intelligence and Driverless Self-Driving Cars,** and **"State-of-the-Art AI Driverless Self-Driving Cars," and "Top Trends in AI Self-Driving Cars," and "AI Innovations and Self-Driving Cars," "Crucial Advances for AI**

Driverless Cars," "Sociotechnical Insights and AI Driverless Cars," "Pioneering Advances for AI Driverless Cars" and "Leading Edge Trends for AI Driverless Cars," "The Cutting Edge of AI Autonomous Cars" and "The Next Wave of AI Self-Driving Cars" and "Revolutionary Innovations of AI Self-Driving Cars," and "AI Self-Driving Cars Breakthroughs," "Trailblazing Trends for AI Self-Driving Cars," "Ingenious Strides for AI Driverless Cars," "AI Self-Driving Cars Inventiveness," "Visionary Secrets of AI Driverless Cars," "Spearheading AI Self-Driving Cars," "Spurring AI Self-Driving Cars," "Avant-Garde AI Driverless Cars," "AI Self-Driving Cars Evolvement," "AI Driverless Cars Chrysalis," "Boosting AI Autonomous Cars," "AI Self-Driving Cars Trendsetting," "AI Autonomous Cars Forefront, "AI Autonomous Cars Emergence," "AI Autonomous Cars Progress," "AI Self-Driving Cars Prognosis," "AI Self-Driving Cars Momentum," "AI Self-Driving Cars Headway," "AI Self-Driving Cars Vicissitude," "AI Self-Driving Cars Autonomy," "AI Driverless Cars Transmutation," "AI Driverless Cars Potentiality," "AI Driverless Cars Realities," "AI Self-Driving Cars Materiality, "AI Self-Driving Cars Accordance," "AI Self-Driving Cars Equanimity" (they are available on Amazon).

For this book, I am going to borrow my introduction from those companion books, since it does a good job of laying out the landscape of self-driving cars and my overall viewpoints on the topic.

INTRODUCTION TO SELF-DRIVING CARS

This is a book about self-driving cars. Someday in the future, we'll all have self-driving cars and this book will perhaps seem antiquated, but right now, we are at the forefront of the self-driving car wave. Daily news bombards us with flashes of new announcements by one car maker or another and leaves the impression that within the next few weeks or maybe months that the self-driving car will be here. A casual non-technical reader would assume from these news flashes that in fact we must be on the cusp of a true self-driving car.

We are still quite a distance from having a true self-driving car. A true self-driving car is akin to a moonshot. In the same manner that getting us to the moon was an incredible feat, likewise, is achieving a true self-driving car. Anybody that suggests or even brashly states that the true self-driving car is nearly here should be viewed with great skepticism. Indeed, you'll see that I often tend to use the word "hogwash" or "crock" when I assess much of the decidedly *fake news* about self-driving cars.

Indeed, I've been writing a popular blog post about self-driving cars and hitting hard on those that try to wave their hands and pretend that we are on the imminent verge of true self-driving cars. For many years, I've been known as the AI Insider. Besides writing about AI, I also develop AI software. I do what I describe. It also gives me insights into what others that are doing AI are really doing versus what it is said they are doing.

Many faithful readers had asked me to pull together my insightful short essays and put them into another book, which you are now holding.

For those of you that have been reading my essays over the years, this collection not only puts them together into one handy package, I also updated the essays and added new material. For those of you that are new to the topic of self-driving cars and AI, I hope you find these essays approachable and informative. I also tend to have a writing style with a bit of a voice, and so you'll see that I am times have a wry sense of humor and poke at conformity.

As a former professor and founder of an AI research lab, I for many years wrote in the formal language of academic writing. I published in referred journals and served as an editor for several AI journals. This writing here is not of the nature, and I have adopted a different and more informal style for these essays. That being said, I also do mention from time-to-time more rigorous material on AI and encourage you all to dig into those deeper and more formal materials if so interested.

I am also an AI practitioner. This means that I write AI software for a living. Currently, I head-up the Cybernetics Self-Driving Car Institute, where we are developing AI software for self-driving cars.

For those of you that are reading this book and have a penchant for writing code, you might consider taking a look at the open source code available for self-driving cars. This is a handy place to start learning how to develop AI for self-driving cars. There are also many new educational courses spring forth. There is a growing body of those wanting to learn about and develop self-driving cars, and a growing body of colleges, labs, and other avenues by which you can learn about self-driving cars.

This book will provide a foundation of aspects that I think will get you ready for those kinds of more advanced training opportunities. If you've already taken those classes, you'll likely find these essays especially interesting as they offer a perspective that I am betting few other instructors or faculty offered to you. These are challenging essays that ask you to think beyond the conventional about self-driving cars.

THE MOTHER OF ALL AI PROJECTS

In June 2017, Apple CEO Tim Cook came out and finally admitted that Apple has been working on a self-driving car. As you'll see in my essays, Apple was enmeshed in secrecy about their self-driving car efforts. We have only been able to read the tea leaves and guess at what Apple has been up to. The notion of an iCar has been floating for quite a while, and self-driving engineers and researchers have been signing tight-lipped Non-Disclosure Agreements (NDA's) to work on projects at Apple that were as shrouded in mystery as any military invasion plans might be.

Tim Cook said something that many others in the Artificial Intelligence (AI) field have been saying, namely, the creation of a self-driving car has got to be the mother of all AI projects. In other words, it is in fact a tremendous moonshot for AI. If a self-driving car can be crafted and the AI works as we hope, it means that we have made incredible strides with AI and that therefore it opens many other worlds of potential breakthrough accomplishments that AI can solve.

Is this hyperbole? Am I just trying to make AI seem like a miracle worker and so provide self-aggrandizing statements for those of us writing the AI software for self-driving cars? No, it is not hyperbole. Developing a true self-driving car is really, really, really hard to do. Let me take a moment to explain why. As a side note, I realize that the Apple CEO is known for at times uttering hyperbole, and he had previously said for example that the year 2012 was "the mother of all years," and he had said that the release of iOS 10 was "the mother of all releases" – all of which does suggest he likes to use the handy "mother of" expression. But, I assure you, in terms of true self-driving cars, he has hit the nail on the head. For sure.

When you think about a moonshot and how we got to the moon, there are some identifiable characteristics and those same aspects can be applied to creating a true self-driving car. You'll notice that I keep putting the word "true" in front of the self-driving car expression. I do so because as per my essay about the various levels of self-driving cars, there are some self-driving cars that are only somewhat of a self-driving car. The somewhat versions are ones that require a human driver to be ready to intervene. In my view, that's not a true self-driving car. A true self-driving car is one that requires no human driver intervention at all. It is a car that can entirely undertake via automation the driving task without any human driver needed. This is the essence of what is known as a Level 5 self-driving car. We are currently at the Level 2 and Level 3 mark, and not yet at Level 5.

Getting to the moon involved aspects such as having big stretch goals, incremental progress, experimentation, innovation, and so on. Let's review how this applied to the moonshot of the bygone era, and how it applies to the self-driving car moonshot of today.

Big Stretch Goal

Trying to take a human and deliver the human to the moon, and bring them back, safely, was an extremely large stretch goal at the time. No one knew whether it could be done. The technology wasn't available yet. The cost was huge. The determination would need to be fierce. Etc. To reach a Level 5 self-driving car is going to be the same. It is a big stretch goal. We can readily get to the Level 3, and we are able to see the Level 4 just up ahead, but a Level 5 is still an unknown as to if it is doable. It should eventually be doable and in the same way that we thought we'd eventually get to the moon, but when it will occur is a different story.

Incremental Progress

Getting to the moon did not happen overnight in one fell swoop. It took years and years of incremental progress to get there. Likewise for self-driving cars. Google has famously been striving to get to the Level 5, and pretty much been willing to forgo dealing with the intervening levels, but most of the other self-driving car makers are doing the incremental route. Let's get a good Level 2 and a somewhat Level 3 going. Then, let's improve the Level 3 and get a somewhat Level 4 going. Then, let's improve the Level 4 and finally arrive at a Level 5. This seems to be the prevalent way that we are going to achieve the true self-driving car.

Experimentation

You likely know that there were various experiments involved in perfecting the approach and technology to get to the moon. As per making incremental progress, we first tried to see if we could get a rocket to go into space and safety return, then put a monkey in there, then with a human, then we went all the way to the moon but didn't land, and finally we arrived at the mission that actually landed on the moon.

Self-driving cars are the same way. We are doing simulations of self-driving cars. We do testing of self-driving cars on private land under controlled situations.

We do testing of self-driving cars on public roadways, often having to meet regulatory requirements including for example having an engineer or equivalent in the car to take over the controls if needed. And so on. Experiments big and small are needed to figure out what works and what doesn't.

Innovation

There are already some advances in AI that are allowing us to progress toward self-driving cars. We are going to need even more advances. Innovation in all aspects of technology are going to be required to achieve a true self-driving car. By no means do we already have everything in-hand that we need to get there. Expect new inventions and new approaches, new algorithms, etc.

Setbacks

Most of the pundits are avoiding talking about potential setbacks in the progress toward self-driving cars. Getting to the moon involved many setbacks, some of which you never have heard of and were buried at the time so as to not dampen enthusiasm and funding for getting to the moon. A recurring theme in many of my included essays is that there are going to be setbacks as we try to arrive at a true self-driving car. Take a deep breath and be ready. I just hope the setbacks don't completely stop progress. I am sure that it will cause progress to alter in a manner that we've not yet seen in the self-driving car field. I liken the self-driving car of today to the excitement everyone had for Uber when it first got going. Today, we have a different view of Uber and with each passing day there are more regulations to the ride sharing business and more concerns raised. The darling child only stays a darling until finally that child acts up. It will happen the same with self-driving cars.

SELF-DRIVING CARS CHALLENGES

But what exactly makes things so hard to have a true self-driving car, you might be asking. You have seen cruise control for years and years. You've lately seen cars that can do parallel parking. You've seen YouTube videos of Tesla drivers that put their hands out the window as their car zooms along the highway, and seen to therefore be in a self-driving car. Aren't we just needing to put a few more sensors onto a car and then we'll have in-hand a true self-driving car? Nope.

Consider for a moment the nature of the driving task. We don't just let anyone at any age drive a car. Worldwide, most countries won't license a driver until the age of 18, though many do allow a learner's permit at the age of 15 or 16. Some suggest that a younger age would be physically too small to reach the controls of the car. Though this might be the case, we could easily adjust the controls to allow for younger aged and thus smaller stature. It's not their physical size that matters. It's their cognitive development that matters.

To drive a car, you need to be able to reason about the car, what the car can and cannot do. You need to know how to operate the car. You need to know about how other cars on the road drive. You need to know what is allowed in driving such as speed limits and driving within marked lanes. You need to be able to react to situations and be able to avoid getting into accidents. You need to ascertain when to hit your brakes, when to steer clear of a pedestrian, and how to keep from ramming that motorcyclist that just cut you off.

Many of us had taken courses on driving. We studied about driving and took driver training. We had to take a test and pass it to be able to drive. The point being that though most adults take the driving task for granted, and we often "mindlessly" drive our cars, there is a significant amount of cognitive effort that goes into driving a car. After a while, it becomes second nature. You don't especially think about how you drive, you just do it. But, if you watch a novice driver, say a teenager learning to drive, you suddenly realize that there is a lot more complexity to it than we seem to realize.

Furthermore, driving is a very serious task. I recall when my daughter and son first learned to drive. They are both very conscientious people. They wanted to make sure that whatever they did, they did well, and that they did not harm anyone. Every day, when you get into a car, it is probably around 4,000 pounds of hefty metal and plastics (about two tons), and it is a lethal weapon. Think about it. You drive down the street in an object that weighs two tons and with the engine it can accelerate and ram into anything you want to hit. The damage a car can inflict is very scary. Both my children were surprised that they were being given the right to maneuver this monster of a beast that could cause tremendous harm entirely by merely letting go of the steering wheel for a moment or taking your eyes off the road.

In fact, in the United States alone there are about 30,000 deaths per year by auto accidents, which is around 100 per day. Given that there are about 263 million cars in the United States, I am actually more amazed that the number of fatalities is not a lot higher.

During my morning commute, I look at all the thousands of cars on the freeway around me, and I think that if all of them decided to go zombie and drive in a crazy maniac way, there would be many people dead. Somehow, incredibly, each day, most people drive relatively safely. To me, that's a miracle right there. Getting millions and millions of people to be safe and sane when behind the wheel of a two ton mobile object, it's a feat that we as a society should admire with pride.

So, hopefully you are in agreement that the driving task requires a great deal of cognition. You don't' need to be especially smart to drive a car, and we've done quite a bit to make car driving viable for even the average dolt. There isn't an IQ test that you need to take to drive a car. If you can read and write, and pass a test, you pretty much can legally drive a car. There are of course some that drive a car and are not legally permitted to do so, plus there are private areas such as farms where drivers are young, but for public roadways in the United States, you can be generally of average intelligence (or less) and be able to legally drive.

This though makes it seem like the cognitive effort must not be much. If the cognitive effort was truly hard, wouldn't we only have Einstein's that could drive a car? We have made sure to keep the driving task as simple as we can, by making the controls easy and relatively standardized, and by having roads that are relatively standardized, and so on. It is as though Disneyland has put their Autopia into the real-world, by us all as a society agreeing that roads will be a certain way, and we'll all abide by the various rules of driving.

A modest cognitive task by a human is still something that stymies AI. You certainly know that AI has been able to beat chess players and be good at other kinds of games. This type of narrow cognition is not what car driving is about. Car driving is much wider. It requires knowledge about the world, which a chess playing AI system does not need to know. The cognitive aspects of driving are on the one hand seemingly simple, but at the same time require layer upon layer of knowledge about cars, people, roads, rules, and a myriad of other "common sense" aspects. We don't have any AI systems today that have that same kind of breadth and depth of awareness and knowledge.

As revealed in my essays, the self-driving car of today is using trickery to do particular tasks. It is all very narrow in operation. Plus, it currently assumes that a human driver is ready to intervene. It is like a child that we have taught to stack blocks, but we are needed to be right there in case the child stacks them too high and they begin to fall over.

AI of today is brittle, it is narrow, and it does not approach the cognitive abilities of humans. This is why the true self-driving car is somewhere out in the future.

Another aspect to the driving task is that it is not solely a mind exercise. You do need to use your senses to drive. You use your eyes a vision sensors to see the road ahead. You vision capability is like a streaming video, which your brain needs to continually analyze as you drive. Where is the road? Is there a pedestrian in the way? Is there another car ahead of you? Your senses are relying a flood of info to your brain. Self-driving cars are trying to do the same, by using cameras, radar, ultrasound, and lasers. This is an attempt at mimicking how humans have senses and sensory apparatus.

Thus, the driving task is mental and physical. You use your senses, you use your arms and legs to manipulate the controls of the car, and you use your brain to assess the sensory info and direct your limbs to act upon the controls of the car. This all happens instantly. If you've ever perhaps gotten something in your eye and only had one eye available to drive with, you suddenly realize how dependent upon vision you are. If you have a broken foot with a cast, you suddenly realize how hard it is to control the brake pedal and the accelerator. If you've taken medication and your brain is maybe sluggish, you suddenly realize how much mental strain is required to drive a car.

An AI system that plays chess only needs to be focused on playing chess. The physical aspects aren't important because usually a human moves the chess pieces or the chessboard is shown on an electronic display. Using AI for a more life-and-death task such as analyzing MRI images of patients, this again does not require physical capabilities and instead is done by examining images of bits.

Driving a car is a true life-and-death task. It is a use of AI that can easily and at any moment produce death. For those colleagues of mine that are developing this AI, as am I, we need to keep in mind the somber aspects of this. We are producing software that will have in its virtual hands the lives of the occupants of the car, and the lives of those in other nearby cars, and the lives of nearby pedestrians, etc. Chess is not usually a life-or-death matter.

Driving is all around us. Cars are everywhere. Most of today's AI applications involve only a small number of people. Or, they are behind the scenes and we as humans have other recourse if the AI messes up. AI that is driving a car at 80 miles per hour on a highway had better not mess up. The consequences are grave.

Multiply this by the number of cars, if we could put magically self-driving into every car in the USA, we'd have AI running in the 263 million cars. That's a lot of AI spread around. This is AI on a massive scale that we are not doing today and that offers both promise and potential peril.

There are some that want AI for self-driving cars because they envision a world without any car accidents. They envision a world in which there is no car congestion and all cars cooperate with each other. These are wonderful utopian visions.

They are also very misleading. The adoption of self-driving cars is going to be incremental and not overnight. We cannot economically just junk all existing cars. Nor are we going to be able to affordably retrofit existing cars. It is more likely that self-driving cars will be built into new cars and that over many years of gradual replacement of existing cars that we'll see the mix of self-driving cars become substantial in the real-world.

In these essays, I have tried to offer technological insights without being overly technical in my description, and also blended the business, societal, and economic aspects too. Technologists need to consider the non-technological impacts of what they do. Non-technologists should be aware of what is being developed.

We all need to work together to collectively be prepared for the enormous disruption and transformative aspects of true self-driving cars.

WHAT THIS BOOK PROVIDES

What does this book provide to you? It introduces many of the key elements about self-driving cars and does so with an AI based perspective. I weave together technical and non-technical aspects, readily going from being concerned about the cognitive capabilities of the driving task and how the technology is embodying this into self-driving cars, and in the next breath I discuss the societal and economic aspects.

They are all intertwined because that's the way reality is. You cannot separate out the technology per se, and instead must consider it within the milieu of what is being invented and innovated, and do so with a mindset towards the contemporary mores and culture that shape what we are doing and what we hope to do.

WHY THIS BOOK

I wrote this book to try and bring to the public view many aspects about self-driving cars that nobody seems to be discussing.

For business leaders that are either involved in making self-driving cars or that are going to leverage self-driving cars, I hope that this book will enlighten you as to the risks involved and ways in which you should be strategizing about how to deal with those risks.

For entrepreneurs, startups and other businesses that want to enter into the self-driving car market that is emerging, I hope this book sparks your interest in doing so, and provides some sense of what might be prudent to pursue.

For researchers that study self-driving cars, I hope this book spurs your interest in the risks and safety issues of self-driving cars, and also nudges you toward conducting research on those aspects.

For students in computer science or related disciplines, I hope this book will provide you with interesting and new ideas and material, for which you might conduct research or provide some career direction insights for you.

For AI companies and high-tech companies pursuing self-driving cars, this book will hopefully broaden your view beyond just the mere coding and development needed to make self-driving cars.

For all readers, I hope that you will find the material in this book to be stimulating. Some of it will be repetitive of things you already know. But I am pretty sure that you'll also find various eureka moments whereby you'll discover a new technique or approach that you had not earlier thought of. I am also betting that there will be material that forces you to rethink some of your current practices.

I am not saying you will suddenly have an epiphany and change what you are doing. I do think though that you will reconsider or perhaps revisit what you are doing.

For anyone choosing to use this book for teaching purposes, please take a look at my suggestions for doing so, as described in the Appendix. I have found the material handy in courses that I have taught, and likewise other faculty have told me that they have found the material handy, in some cases as extended readings and in other instances as a core part of their course (depending on the nature of the class).

In my writing for this book, I have tried carefully to blend both the practitioner and the academic styles of writing.

It is not as abstract as is typical academic journal writing, but at the same time offers depth by going into the nuances and trade-offs of various practices.

The word "deep" is in vogue today, meaning getting deeply into a subject or topic, and so is the word "unpack" which means to tease out the underlying aspects of a subject or topic. I have sought to offer material that addresses an issue or topic by going relatively deeply into it and make sure that it is well unpacked.

In any book about AI, it is difficult to use our everyday words without having some of them be misinterpreted. Specifically, it is easy to anthropomorphize AI. When I say that an AI system "knows" something, I do not want you to construe that the AI system has sentience and "knows" in the same way that humans do. They aren't that way, as yet. I have tried to use quotes around such words from time-to-time to emphasize that the words I am using should not be misinterpreted to ascribe true human intelligence to the AI systems that we know of today. If I used quotes around all such words, the book would be very difficult to read, and so I am doing so judiciously. Please keep that in mind as you read the material, thanks.

Some of the material is time-based in terms of covering underway activities, and though some of it might decay, nonetheless I believe you'll find the material useful and informative.

COMPANION BOOKS BY DR. ELIOT

1. **"Introduction to Driverless Self-Driving Cars"** by Dr. Lance Eliot
2. **"Innovation and Thought Leadership on Self-Driving Driverless Cars"**
3. **"Advances in AI and Autonomous Vehicles: Cybernetic Self-Driving Cars"**
4. **"Self-Driving Cars: The Mother of All AI Projects"** by Dr. Lance Eliot
5. **"New Advances in AI Autonomous Driverless Self-Driving Cars"**
6. **"Autonomous Vehicle Driverless Self-Driving Cars and Artificial Intelligence"** by Dr. Lance Eliot and Michael B. Eliot
7. **"Transformative Artificial Intelligence Driverless Self-Driving Cars"**
8. **"Disruptive Artificial Intelligence and Driverless Self-Driving Cars"**
9. "State-of-the-Art AI Driverless Self-Driving Cars" by Dr. Lance Eliot
10. "Top Trends in AI Self-Driving Cars" by Dr. Lance Eliot
11. **"AI Innovations and Self-Driving Cars"** by Dr. Lance Eliot
12. **"Crucial Advances for AI Driverless Cars"** by Dr. Lance Eliot
13. **"Sociotechnical Insights and AI Driverless Cars"** by Dr. Lance Eliot.
14. **"Pioneering Advances for AI Driverless Cars"** by Dr. Lance Eliot
15. **"Leading Edge Trends for AI Driverless Cars"** by Dr. Lance Eliot
16. **"The Cutting Edge of AI Autonomous Cars"** by Dr. Lance Eliot
17. **"The Next Wave of AI Self-Driving Cars"** by Dr. Lance Eliot
18. **"Revolutionary Innovations of AI Driverless Cars"** by Dr. Lance Eliot
19. **"AI Self-Driving Cars Breakthroughs"** by Dr. Lance Eliot
20. **"Trailblazing Trends for AI Self-Driving Cars"** by Dr. Lance Eliot
21. **"Ingenious Strides for AI Driverless Cars"** by Dr. Lance Eliot
22. **"AI Self-Driving Cars Inventiveness"** by Dr. Lance Eliot
23. **"Visionary Secrets of AI Driverless Cars"** by Dr. Lance Eliot
24. **"Spearheading AI Self-Driving Cars"** by Dr. Lance Eliot
25. **"Spurring AI Self-Driving Cars"** by Dr. Lance Eliot
26. **"Avant-Garde AI Driverless Cars"** by Dr. Lance Eliot
27. **"AI Self-Driving Cars Evolvement"** by Dr. Lance Eliot
28. **"AI Driverless Cars Chrysalis"** by Dr. Lance Eliot
29. **"Boosting AI Autonomous Cars"** by Dr. Lance Eliot
30. **"AI Self-Driving Cars Trendsetting"** by Dr. Lance Eliot
31. **"AI Autonomous Cars Forefront"** by Dr. Lance Eliot
32. **"AI Autonomous Cars Emergence"** by Dr. Lance Eliot
33. **"AI Autonomous Cars Progress"** by Dr. Lance Eliot
34. **"AI Self-Driving Cars Prognosis"** by Dr. Lance Eliot
35. **"AI Self-Driving Cars Momentum"** by Dr. Lance Eliot
36. **"AI Self-Driving Cars Headway"** by Dr. Lance Eliot
37. **"AI Self-Driving Cars Vicissitude"** by Dr. Lance Eliot
38. **"AI Self-Driving Cars Autonomy"** by Dr. Lance Eliot
39. **"AI Driverless Cars Transmutation"** by Dr. Lance Eliot
40. **"AI Driverless Cars Potentiality"** by Dr. Lance Eliot
41. **"AI Driverless Cars Realities"** by Dr. Lance Eliot
42. **"AI Self-Driving Cars Materiality"** by Dr. Lance Eliot
43. **"AI Self-Driving Cars Accordance"** by Dr. Lance Eliot
44. **"AI Self-Driving Cars Equanimity"** by Dr. Lance Eliot

These books are available on Amazon and at other major global booksellers.

CHAPTER 1

ELIOT FRAMEWORK FOR AI SELF-DRIVING CARS

CHAPTER 1

ELIOT FRAMEWORK FOR AI SELF-DRIVING CARS

This chapter is a core foundational aspect for understanding AI self-driving cars and I have used this same chapter in several of my other books to introduce the reader to essential elements of this field. Once you've read this chapter, you'll be prepared to read the rest of the material since the foundational essence of the components of autonomous AI driverless self-driving cars will have been established for you.

When I give presentations about self-driving cars and teach classes on the topic, I have found it helpful to provide a framework around which the various key elements of self-driving cars can be understood and organized (see diagram at the end of this chapter). The framework needs to be simple enough to convey the overarching elements, but at the same time not so simple that it belies the true complexity of self-driving cars. As such, I am going to describe the framework here and try to offer in a thousand words (or more!) what the framework diagram itself intends to portray.

The core elements on the diagram are numbered for ease of reference. The numbering does not suggest any kind of prioritization of the elements. Each element is crucial. Each element has a purpose, and otherwise would not be included in the framework. For some self-driving cars, a particular element might be more important or somehow distinguished in comparison to other self-driving cars.

You could even use the framework to rate a particular self-driving car, doing so by gauging how well it performs in each of the elements of the framework. I will describe each of the elements, one at a time. After doing so, I'll discuss aspects that illustrate how the elements interact and perform during the overall effort of a self-driving car.

At the AI Self-Driving Car Institute, we use the framework to keep track of what we are working on, and how we are developing software that fills in what is needed to achieve Level 5 self-driving cars.

D-01: Sensor Capture

Let's start with the one element that often gets the most attention in the press about self-driving cars, namely, the sensory devices for a self-driving car.

On the framework, the box labeled as D-01 indicates "Sensor Capture" and refers to the processes of the self-driving car that involve collecting data from the myriad of sensors that are used for a self-driving car. The types of devices typically involved are listed, such as the use of mono cameras, stereo cameras, LIDAR devices, radar systems, ultrasonic devices, GPS, IMU, and so on.

These devices are tasked with obtaining data about the status of the self-driving car and the world around it. Some of the devices are continually providing updates, while others of the devices await an indication by the self-driving car that the device is supposed to collect data. The data might be first transformed in some fashion by the device itself, or it might instead be fed directly into the sensor capture as raw data. At that point, it might be up to the sensor capture processes to do transformations on the data. This all varies depending upon the nature of the devices being used and how the devices were designed and developed.

D-02: Sensor Fusion

Imagine that your eyeballs receive visual images, your nose receives odors, your ears receive sounds, and in essence each of your distinct sensory devices is getting some form of input. The input befits the nature of the device. Likewise, for a self-driving car, the cameras provide visual images, the radar returns radar reflections, and so on. Each device provides the data as befits what the device does.

At some point, using the analogy to humans, you need to merge together what your eyes see, what your nose smells, what your ears hear, and piece it all together into a larger sense of what the world is all about and what is happening around you. Sensor fusion is the action of taking the singular aspects from each of the devices and putting them together into a larger puzzle.

Sensor fusion is a tough task. There are some devices that might not be working at the time of the sensor capture. Or, there might some devices that are unable to report well what they have detected. Again, using a human analogy, suppose you are in a dark room and so your eyes cannot see much. At that point, you might need to rely more so on your ears and what you hear. The same is true for a self-driving car. If the cameras are obscured due to snow and sleet, it might be that the radar can provide a greater indication of what the external conditions consist of.

In the case of a self-driving car, there can be a plethora of such sensory devices. Each is reporting what it can. Each might have its difficulties. Each might have its limitations, such as how far ahead it can detect an object. All of these limitations need to be considered during the sensor fusion task.

D-03: Virtual World Model

For humans, we presumably keep in our minds a model of the world around us when we are driving a car. In your mind, you know that the car is going at say 60 miles per hour and that you are on a freeway.

You have a model in your mind that your car is surrounded by other cars, and that there are lanes to the freeway. Your model is not only based on what you can see, hear, etc., but also what you know about the nature of the world. You know that at any moment that car ahead of you can smash on its brakes, or the car behind you can ram into your car, or that the truck in the next lane might swerve into your lane.

The AI of the self-driving car needs to have a virtual world model, which it then keeps updated with whatever it is receiving from the sensor fusion, which received its input from the sensor capture and the sensory devices.

D-04: System Action Plan

By having a virtual world model, the AI of the self-driving car is able to keep track of where the car is and what is happening around the car. In addition, the AI needs to determine what to do next. Should the self-driving car hit its brakes? Should the self-driving car stay in its lane or swerve into the lane to the left? Should the self-driving car accelerate or slow down?

A system action plan needs to be prepared by the AI of the self-driving car. The action plan specifies what actions should be taken. The actions need to pertain to the status of the virtual world model. Plus, the actions need to be realizable.

This realizability means that the AI cannot just assert that the self-driving car should suddenly sprout wings and fly. Instead, the AI must be bound by whatever the self-driving car can actually do, such as coming to a halt in a distance of X feet at a speed of Y miles per hour, rather than perhaps asserting that the self-driving car come to a halt in 0 feet as though it could instantaneously come to a stop while it is in motion.

D-05: Controls Activation

The system action plan is implemented by activating the controls of the car to act according to what the plan stipulates.

This might mean that the accelerator control is commanded to increase the speed of the car. Or, the steering control is commanded to turn the steering wheel 30 degrees to the left or right.

One question arises as to whether or not the controls respond as they are commanded to do. In other words, suppose the AI has commanded the accelerator to increase, but for some reason it does not do so. Or, maybe it tries to do so, but the speed of the car does not increase. The controls activation feeds back into the virtual world model, and simultaneously the virtual world model is getting updated from the sensors, the sensor capture, and the sensor fusion. This allows the AI to ascertain what has taken place as a result of the controls being commanded to take some kind of action.

By the way, please keep in mind that though the diagram seems to have a linear progression to it, the reality is that these are all aspects of the self-driving car that are happening in parallel and simultaneously. The sensors are capturing data, meanwhile the sensor fusion is taking place, meanwhile the virtual model is being updated, meanwhile the system action plan is being formulated and reformulated, meanwhile the controls are being activated.

This is the same as a human being that is driving a car. They are eyeballing the road, meanwhile they are fusing in their mind the sights, sounds, etc., meanwhile their mind is updating their model of the world around them, meanwhile they are formulating an action plan of what to do, and meanwhile they are pushing their foot onto the pedals and steering the car. In the normal course of driving a car, you are doing all of these at once. I mention this so that when you look at the diagram, you will think of the boxes as processes that are all happening at the same time, and not as though only one happens and then the next.

They are shown diagrammatically in a simplistic manner to help comprehend what is taking place. You though should also realize that they are working in parallel and simultaneous with each other. This is a tough aspect in that the inter-element communications involve latency and other aspects that must be taken into account.

There can be delays in one element updating and then sharing its latest status with other elements.

D-06: Automobile & CAN

Contemporary cars use various automotive electronics and a Controller Area Network (CAN) to serve as the components that underlie the driving aspects of a car. There are Electronic Control Units (ECU's) which control subsystems of the car, such as the engine, the brakes, the doors, the windows, and so on.

The elements D-01, D-02, D-03, D-04, D-05 are layered on top of the D-06, and must be aware of the nature of what the D-06 is able to do and not do.

D-07: In-Car Commands

Humans are going to be occupants in self-driving cars. In a Level 5 self-driving car, there must be some form of communication that takes place between the humans and the self-driving car. For example, I go into a self-driving car and tell it that I want to be driven over to Disneyland, and along the way I want to stop at In-and-Out Burger. The self-driving car now parses what I've said and tries to then establish a means to carry out my wishes.

In-car commands can happen at any time during a driving journey. Though my example was about an in-car command when I first got into my self-driving car, it could be that while the self-driving car is carrying out the journey that I change my mind. Perhaps after getting stuck in traffic, I tell the self-driving car to forget about getting the burgers and just head straight over to the theme park. The self-driving car needs to be alert to in-car commands throughout the journey.

D-08: V2X Communications

We will ultimately have self-driving cars communicating with each other, doing so via V2V (Vehicle-to-Vehicle) communications.

We will also have self-driving cars that communicate with the roadways and other aspects of the transportation infrastructure, doing so via V2I (Vehicle-to-Infrastructure).

The variety of ways in which a self-driving car will be communicating with other cars and infrastructure is being called V2X, whereby the letter X means whatever else we identify as something that a car should or would want to communicate with. The V2X communications will be taking place simultaneous with everything else on the diagram, and those other elements will need to incorporate whatever it gleans from those V2X communications.

D-09: Deep Learning

The use of Deep Learning permeates all other aspects of the self-driving car. The AI of the self-driving car will be using deep learning to do a better job at the systems action plan, and at the control's activation, and at the sensor fusion, and so on.

Currently, the use of artificial neural networks is the most prevalent form of deep learning. Based on large swaths of data, the neural networks attempt to "learn" from the data and therefore direct the efforts of the self-driving car accordingly.

D-10: Tactical AI

Tactical AI is the element of dealing with the moment-to-moment driving of the self-driving car. Is the self-driving car staying in its lane of the freeway? Is the car responding appropriately to the controls commands? Are the sensory devices working?

For human drivers, the tactical equivalent can be seen when you watch a novice driver such as a teenager that is first driving. They are focused on the mechanics of the driving task, keeping their eye on the road while also trying to properly control the car.

D-11: Strategic AI

The Strategic AI aspects of a self-driving car are dealing with the larger picture of what the self-driving car is trying to do. If I had asked that the self-driving car take me to Disneyland, there is an overall journey map that needs to be kept and maintained.

There is an interaction between the Strategic AI and the Tactical AI. The Strategic AI is wanting to keep on the mission of the driving, while the Tactical AI is focused on the particulars underway in the driving effort. If the Tactical AI seems to wander away from the overarching mission, the Strategic AI wants to see why and get things back on track. If the Tactical AI realizes that there is something amiss on the self-driving car, it needs to alert the Strategic AI accordingly and have an adjustment to the overarching mission that is underway.

D-12: Self-Aware AI

Very few of the self-driving cars being developed are including a Self-Aware AI element, which we at the Cybernetic Self-Driving Car Institute believe is crucial to Level 5 self-driving cars.

The Self-Aware AI element is intended to watch over itself, in the sense that the AI is making sure that the AI is working as intended. Suppose you had a human driving a car, and they were starting to drive erratically. Hopefully, their own self-awareness would make them realize they themselves are driving poorly, such as perhaps starting to fall asleep after having been driving for hours on end. If you had a passenger in the car, they might be able to alert the driver if the driver is starting to do something amiss.

This is exactly what the Self-Aware AI element tries to do, it becomes the overseer of the AI, and tries to detect when the AI has become faulty or confused, and then find ways to overcome the issue.

D-13: Economic

The economic aspects of a self-driving car are not per se a technology aspect of a self-driving car, but the economics do indeed impact the nature of a self-driving car. For example, the cost of outfitting a self-driving car with every kind of possible sensory device is prohibitive, and so choices need to be made about which devices are used. And, for those sensory devices chosen, whether they would have a full set of features or a more limited set of features.

We are going to have self-driving cars that are at the low-end of a consumer cost point, and others at the high-end of a consumer cost point. You cannot expect that the self-driving car at the low-end is going to be as robust as the one at the high-end. I realize that many of the self-driving car pundits are acting as though all self-driving cars will be the same, but they won't be. Just like anything else, we are going to have self-driving cars that have a range of capabilities. Some will be better than others. Some will be safer than others. This is the way of the real-world, and so we need to be thinking about the economics aspects when considering the nature of self-driving cars.

D-14: Societal

This component encompasses the societal aspects of AI which also impacts the technology of self-driving cars. For example, the famous Trolley Problem involves what choices should a self-driving car make when faced with life-and-death matters. If the self-driving car is about to either hit a child standing in the roadway, or instead ram into a tree at the side of the road and possibly kill the humans in the self-driving car, which choice should be made?

We need to keep in mind the societal aspects will underlie the AI of the self-driving car. Whether we are aware of it explicitly or not, the AI will have embedded into it various societal assumptions.

D-15: Innovation

I included the notion of innovation into the framework because we can anticipate that whatever a self-driving car consists of, it will continue to be innovated over time. The self-driving cars coming out in the next several years will undoubtedly be different and less innovative than the versions that come out in ten years hence, and so on.

Framework Overall

For those of you that want to learn about self-driving cars, you can potentially pick a particular element and become specialized in that aspect. Some engineers are focusing on the sensory devices. Some engineers focus on the controls activation. And so on. There are specialties in each of the elements.

Researchers are likewise specializing in various aspects. For example, there are researchers that are using Deep Learning to see how best it can be used for sensor fusion. There are other researchers that are using Deep Learning to derive good System Action Plans. Some are studying how to develop AI for the Strategic aspects of the driving task, while others are focused on the Tactical aspects.

A well-prepared all-around software developer that is involved in self-driving cars should be familiar with all of the elements, at least to the degree that they know what each element does. This is important since whatever piece of the pie that the software developer works on, they need to be knowledgeable about what the other elements are doing.

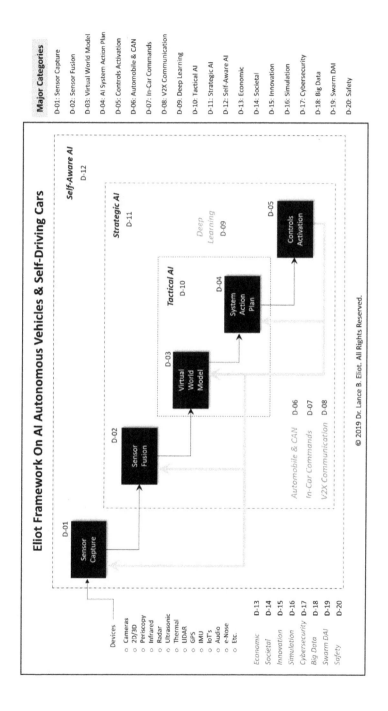

Eliot Framework On AI Autonomous Vehicles & Self-Driving Cars

Major Categories

D-01: Sensor Capture
D-02: Sensor Fusion
D-03: Virtual World Model
D-04: AI System Action Plan
D-05: Controls Activation
D-06: Automobile & CAN
D-07: In-Car Commands
D-08: V2X Communication
D-09: Deep Learning
D-10: Tactical AI
D-11: Strategic AI
D-12: Self-Aware AI
D-13: Economic
D-14: Societal
D-15: Innovation
D-16: Simulation
D-17: Cybersecurity
D-18: Big Data
D-19: Swarm DAI
D-20: Safety

CHAPTER 2
AI OLIGOPOLIES
AND
AI SELF-DRIVING CARS

CHAPTER 2
AI OLOGOPOLIES
AND AI SELF-DRIVING CARS

Artificial Intelligence (AI) systems are increasingly being deployed into all facets of our existence.

Via the advent of Machine Learning (ML) and Deep Learning (DL), many of these AI applications are intended to adjust on-the-fly and tailor themselves in real-time to the efforts they were designed to meet.

Rather than one size fits all, AI offers the potential for a mantra that says automation ought to always fit the size needed, including at the time of the need and as the need so arises.

The good news is that these newer AI implementations tend to hone in on our needs and can become essential to our daily lives.

It is a bit of a slippery slope, lamentably, involving us wanting AI that can do more for us, and meanwhile, we become perhaps overly addicted and dependent upon such AI systems.

Most of the time, you don't particularly care who makes the AI and only are focused on whether it provides the value that you are seeking. If the AI was made by a large conglomerate, fine, while if devised by somebody in their comfy pajamas while in their one-bedroom makeshift office, that's perfectly okay too.

There is a rub though to this ownership and promulgator notion.

Some are concerned that we are going to end up in a situation whereby only a handful of entities will control the AI systems that gradually become an essential and seemingly irreplaceable part of our lives.

Within the hands of a few might become an undue concentration of power.

And as per the immortal words of Sir John Emerich Edward Dalberg-Action in 1887, power tends to corrupt, while absolute power corrupts absolutely.

There is a rising tide of concern that state-of-the-art AI is heading toward a type of oligopoly, meaning that the markets served by AI will be dominated by a small number of firms. This, in turn, portends that those firms might be able to dictate to all of us what the AI does, along with how much we must pay to use the AI, and how and who can benefit from the AI, etc.

If you believe in the economic and societal theories underlying oligopolies, essentially it is a "bad" thing for consumers when a small set of firms dominate a market, partially due to the lack of abject competition and the lopsided power grab enabled by those companies.

Let's be clear and agree that this does not imply that there will be only a handful of gigantic companies that serve us all of the myriad types of AI systems that are and will continue to emerge.

Instead, imagine that we are heading toward a sea of AI oligopolies, a veritable cabal of distinct oligopolistic instances, each focused on a particular AI aimed niche.

For example, as will be noted shortly, the emergence of AI-based self-driving cars would appear to be a fast-approaching AI oligopoly, and for which few realize the importance and significance this foreshadows.

That being said, oligopolies are not some arcane and infrequent construct.

Most would agree that today's social media is dominated by a handful of entrenched firms, regardless of any AI-related matters and simply as an evidentiary exemplar of how we already exist in the midst of notable oligopolistic circumstances.

For years and years, the film and television industry has been cited as a form of oligopoly.

There is more, a lot more of such examples.

Few tend to realize that in the wireless carrier marketspace, only four companies amount to nearly 98% of that specific industry, meanwhile consumer rights group clamor and bemoan the fact that there are few other viable choices to select from.

In an ongoing and quite acrimonious debate, there are those that argue that the U.S. domestic airline industry is an oligopoly. You might be shocked to think so, and yet the numbers show that a mere four airlines constitute over 80% of the flights by domestic passengers.

Overall, we today find ourselves surrounded by and enmeshed in a complicated world of innumerable oligopolies.

In that case, perhaps the furor over the soon upon us AI-oligopolies is misplaced since it constitutes presumably nothing extraordinary and perhaps doesn't deserve any outsized attention or complaint.

Well, just because you happened to wallow in mud before does not ergo mean that you should necessarily accept it in the future, goes the counter-argument. Time to get out of the murk and clean things up.

Furthermore, the AI oligopolies are sneakier, some assert, and we are already foolishly letting the horse out of the barn, or the proverbial genie out of the bottle, all of which could be dealt with now, rather than suffering the repercussions later on and having to solve a problem that should not have festered and been permitted to emerge.

AI oligopolies are predicted to surface in a multitude of areas such as AI in the medical domain, AI in the financial sector, AI in the law, and so on.

Here's today's interesting question: *Will AI-based true self-driving cars be led and dominated by a handful of firms and thus constitutes a pending formation of an AI oligopoly that is about to arise?*

Let's unpack the matter and see.

The Levels Of Self-Driving Cars

True self-driving cars are ones that the AI drives the car entirely on its own and there isn't any human assistance during the driving task.

These driverless vehicles are considered a Level 4 and Level 5, while a car that requires a human driver to co-share the driving effort is usually considered at a Level 2 or Level 3. The cars that co-share the driving task are described as being semi-autonomous, and typically contain a variety of automated add-on's that are referred to as ADAS (Advanced Driver-Assistance Systems).

There is not yet a true self-driving car at Level 5, which we don't yet even know if this will be possible to achieve, and nor how long it will take to get there.

Meanwhile, the Level 4 efforts are gradually trying to get some traction by undergoing very narrow and selective public roadway trials, though there is controversy over whether this testing should be allowed per se (we are all life-or-death guinea pigs in an experiment taking place on our highways and byways, some point out).

Since semi-autonomous cars require a human driver, the adoption of those types of cars won't be markedly different than driving conventional vehicles, so there's not much new per se to cover about them on this topic (though, as you'll see in a moment, the points next made are generally applicable).

For semi-autonomous cars, it is important that the public needs to be forewarned about a disturbing aspect that's been arising lately, namely that in spite of those human drivers that keep posting videos of themselves falling asleep at the wheel of a Level 2 or Level 3 car, we all need to avoid being misled into believing that the driver can take away their attention from the driving task while driving a semi-autonomous car.

You are the responsible party for the driving actions of the vehicle, regardless of how much automation might be tossed into a Level 2 or Level 3.

Self-Driving Cars And AI Oligopolies

For Level 4 and Level 5 true self-driving vehicles, there won't be a human driver involved in the driving task.

All occupants will be passengers.

The AI is doing the driving.

Pundits tend to emphasize that by having AI doing our driving, we are going to hopefully reduce the annual carnage that takes place, which in the United State alone amounts to some 40,000 lives lost in car crashes and an additional 2.3 million people injured via car incidents. The belief is that AI self-driving cars will be safer drivers, mitigating the human foibles of driving such as when driving drunk, distracted driving, and the rest.

What could be wrong with that virtuous desire?

Assuming such a prognostication comes true, it certainly appears to be an unquestionably desirable future.

Recall earlier that I mentioned we oftentimes do not know and nor tend to think about the promulgators of the systems that we use or depend upon?

The same might be said of the emerging field of AI true self-driving cars.

Here's what some insiders are worried about.

Currently, there are perhaps a dozen to two dozen noteworthy firms that are vying toward making true self-driving cars, meaning that they are devising the AI systems that underly having a car be able to perform autonomous self-driving acts.

Industry watchers are anticipating that not all of those striving to such a vaunted goal will productively make it to their AI-based self-driving car dreams, and thus many will essentially fall by the wayside during that painstaking and costly journey.

This doesn't necessarily suggest that those let-downs will all go out of business, though some might, but that they will give up on their AI efforts and aim to deal with self-driving cars when and if they actually emerge.

In the end, there will only be a handful left standing, it is argued, and those such firms will constitute the AI oligopoly of the upcoming self-driving era.

Is this a good thing or a bad thing?

As pointed out, oligopolies are generally considered economically and societally to be undesirable, and we might sensibly assume the same could apply to the niche of self-driving cars.

What could go awry if there is an AI oligopoly in the AI-based self-driving car arena?

Some worry that the roving eye of self-driving cars is going to become a tremendous privacy nightmare.

I have been referring to the aspect that self-driving cars will be roaming along our streets and 24 x 7 capturing video of whatever they see as a kind of roving eye (see my analysis at **this link here**).

Ponder for a moment all of the cars that go past your home on a daily basis in your quiet and innocuous neighborhood, or cars that drive along downtown streets nonstop during the light of day and at nighttime, and assume that all of those cars will have a slew of cameras that are incessantly videotaping anything and everything around them.

Now, take all of that eye-popping video, collect it together via the facet that self-driving cars will be likely arranged into fleets, and are able to easily upload their data via OTA (Over-The-Air) electronic communication into the cloud.

You could even have disparate fleets that decide to share their collected info among their clandestine cabal.

Altogether, if you started to stitch that voluminous data into a formative whole, it provides an incredibly Big Brother akin capability, the likes of which we cannot readily today fathom.

And who will decide how that vast trove of data will be used?

Apparently, the AI oligopoly that is controlling the AI-based self-driving cars.

Should the few that are holding those reins be the ones to decide such weighty matters?

That's one example of a qualm about AI-based self-driving cars.

Take another example, one that deals with access to the use of self-driving cars.

Some proponents of AI-based true self-driving cars are hoping that we will witness a boom in mobility, especially by providing access to those that are today mobility disadvantaged. Our world is currently one of mobility constraints and barriers, while in the future, by embracing self-driving cars, presumably there will be a treasured mobility-for-all existence.

Yet, suppose that the AI self-driving car firms decide that only the wealthy and the well-to-do are going to be permitted to use self-driving cars?

Indeed, some have been wringing their hands that self-driving cars will be solely for the elite and won't reach others that desperately are in need of mobility.

All told, there are plentiful nightmare scenarios about the deployment and access of AI-based self-driving cars, and for which an underlying prevailing fear is that an AI oligopoly might rule the day in this realm.

Actions To Consider

Of course, not everyone agrees that we are heading toward a doomsday AI oligopoly scenario, not in self-driving cars and nor in other AI areas that are being pursued.

There are those that say the AI oligopoly is a false boogieman, and we ought not to be overly reactive whenever the bell is rung about the pitfalls and perils of oligopolies.

In any case, what could be done to either avoid the potential for adverse consequences or possibly deal with any adversity that actually arises from AI oligopolies?

Here are the typical levers and approaches used when coping with an AI oligopoly:

1) Ignore it, live with it as is
2) Wait, watch, and see what happens
3) Monitor stridently, prepare to act
4) Impose controls
5) Force diffusion
6) Break-up altogether
7) Takeover

The first listed aspect, namely, simply ignore the matter, can happen by default, and we might later on wake-up and regret our having been asleep at the wheel, as it were. On the other hand, it could be that an AI oligopoly is a tempest in a teapot and will not ultimately emerge as a quandary, thus why waste time and energy fretting about it.

Some would vehemently say that we ought to at least be doing the second item on the list and be on our guard, watching, waiting, and sniffing around to make sure that an AI oligopoly doesn't start to go into a power-mad mode.

The third item on the list is being on our guard with weapons loaded, ready to take action if or when the AI oligopoly goes askew.

The fourth through the seventh item on the list entails taking overt action about the AI oligopoly. As a society, we could impose regulatory controls, or we could force the firms to share their AI source code and try to diffuse the cabal, and if it came down to it there is the option of breaking up the concentrated ownership or even taking the somewhat Draconian act of a takeover of the AI technology.

Any of the aforementioned approaches need to be assessed and adjudged as per the specific AI oligopoly and the situational context thereof.

Conclusion

Yes, the AI oligopolies are on their way.

They will occur in any number of domains and fields.

Some suggest that if we as a society were to take "suppressive" action now, doing so would likely undercut the zeal by those firms pursuing advances in AI. We might shoot our own foot and derail AI tech that would have otherwise blossomed and helped us in untold ways.

Of course, there are AI conspiracists that insist the AI will someday become sentient and reach the point of singularity and go beyond what we as humans intended the AI to do.

One wonders, if that does occur, would the resultant AI be appreciative to the AI oligopolists that spawned their existence, or might the AI decide those cabal landlords ought to be the first to go.

Well, maybe that's something those AI oligopolists of today might be staying awake at night worrying about and possibly be spurred toward being more charitable and benevolent about their praised AI, now, prior to the day that the AI overlords command all of humanity.

Sleep tight on that dreamy notion.

.

CHAPTER 3
AI INTENT
AND
AI SELF-DRIVING CARS

CHAPTER 3

AI INTENT
AND
AI SELF-DRIVING CARS

Let's start with a bit of a game or puzzle if you will.

These remarks all have something in common:
- The devil made me do it
- I didn't mean to be mean to you
- Something just came over me
- I wanted to do it
- You got what was coming to you
- My motives were pure

What's that all about?

I'll wait a moment for you to ponder the matter.

Okay, now that you gave that some thought, you could answer that those are all various ways in which someone might express their intent or intentions.

In some instances, the person is seemingly expressing their intent directly, while in other cases they appear to be avoiding being pinned down on their own intentions and are trying to toss the intent onto the shoulders of someone or something else.

When we express our intent, there is no particular reason to necessarily believe that it is true per se.

A person can tell you their intentions and yet be lying through their teeth.

Or, a person can offer their intentions and genuinely believe that they are forthcoming in their indication, and yet it might be entirely fabricated and concocted as a kind of rationalization after-the-fact.

Consider too that a person might be offering acrid cynical remarks, for which their intention is buried or hidden within their words, and you accordingly need to somehow decipher or tease out the real meaning of their quips.

There is also the straightforward possibility that the person is utterly clueless about their own intention, and thus are unable to precisely state what their intent is.

And so on.

This naturally leads us to contemplate what intent or intention purports to consist of.

The common definition of intent or intention is that it involves the act of determining something that you want and plan to do, and usually emphasizes that the effort of "intent" encompasses mentally determining upon some action or result.

By referring to the mind or mental processing, the word "intent" opens quite a Pandora's box.

Simply stated, there is no ironclad way to know what someone's mind contains or did contain.

We do not have any means to directly and fully interrogate the brain and have it showcase to us the origins of thoughts and how they came to exist. Our brains and our minds are locked away in our skulls, and the only path to figuring out what is going on consists of poking around from the outside or marginally so from the inside.

Now, yes, you can try using an MRI and other techniques to try and gauge the electromagnetic or biochemical activity of the brain, but be clear that this is a far cry from being able to connect-the-dots directly and be able to definitively indicate that this thought or that thought was derived from these neurons and those neurons.

We have not yet reversed engineered the brain sufficiently to make those kinds of uncontestable proclamations.

Overall, one could even argue that the whole concept of intent and intentions is somewhat obtuse and perhaps a construct of what we want to believe about our actions. Some would say that we want to believe that we do things for a reason, and therefore we offer that there is this thing called "intent" and thus it offers a rational explanation for what otherwise might be nothing of the kind.

For those that relish debating about the topic of free will, perhaps none of us have any capability of intent and we are all pre-programmed to carry out acts, none of which relates to any personal intent and we are simply acting as puppets on a string.

I don't want to go too far off the rails here but did want to mention the philosophical viewpoint that intent might not exist in any ordinary manner and we cannot assume as such that it does.

Since we are on a roll here about thinking widely, there is a handy catchphrase about intent from George Bernard Shaw that offers additional food for thought: "We know there is intention and purpose in the universe, because there is intention and purpose in us."

Notice that this is quite reassuring, namely that since we generally believe that there is intention within us, ergo this somehow implies that there is an intention in the universe, and therefore we are able to remain sanguine and be comforted that everything has a meaning and intention (though some might counterargue that the universe and we are all completely random and purposeless).

While we are on teetering on the edge of this precipice, let's keep going.

Maybe intent and intention is really a cover-up for the acts of humanity.

If you do something adverse, the intent might be a means to placate others about your dastardly deed and act as a distractor from the act committed.

On the other hand, maybe your act was well-intended, yet it led to something adverse, inadvertently and not by design, therefore your intention ought to be given due weight and consideration.

Time to quote another fascinating insight about intent, this one by the revered George Washington: "A man's intentions should be allowed in some respects to plead for his actions."

Note that Washington's quote refers to man's intentions, but we can reasonably allow the meaning to include all of mankind, making the quote to encompass both men and women, restated as a person's intentions should be allowed in some respects to plead for their actions.

Overall, mankind certainly seems to have accepted the stark and generally unchallenged belief that there are intentions and that those intentions are crucial to the acts we undertake.

That being the case, what else has intentions?

Does your beloved pet dog or cat have intentions?

Do all animals have intentions of one kind or another?

There is an acrimonious debate about the idea that animals can form intentions.

Some say that it is obviously the case that they do, while others contend that they quite obviously cannot do so. The usual basis for arguing that animals cannot have intentions is that they mentally are too limited and that only humans have the mental capacity to form intent or intentions. Be careful making that brash claim to any dog or cat lover.

Can a toaster have an intention?

I ask because the other day, my toaster burnt my toast.

Did the toaster do so intentionally, or was it an unintentional act?

You might be irked at such a question and immediately recoil that the toaster obviously lacks any semblance of intent. It is merely a mindless machine that makes toast.

There isn't any there, there.

Without the ingredient or essential component of mental processing, you would seem to be hard-pressed to ascribe intent to something so ordinary and mechanical.

This brings us to a most intriguing twist and the <u>intended</u> focus of this discussion, namely, where does AI fit into this murky matter of intent and intention.

AI systems are increasingly becoming a vital part of our lives.

There are AI systems that do life-impacting diagnoses of X-ray charts and seem to discern whether there is disease present. There are AI systems that decide whether you can get a car loan that you wanted to obtain. Etc.

Is AI more akin to humans and therefore able to form intent, or is AI more similar to a toaster and unable to have any substance of intent?

Lest you think this is an entirely abstract point and not worthy of real-world attention, consider the legal ramifications of whether AI is able to form intent and whether this is noteworthy or not.

In our approach to jurisprudence, we give a tremendous amount of importance to intent, sometimes referred to as scienter in legal circles, and in criminal law make use of intent to ascertain the nature of the crime that can be assigned and the penalty that might ride with the crime undertaken.

As such, this AI-related intent insight by a legal research scholar seems especially apt here: "Because intent tests often serve as a gatekeeper, limiting the scope of claims, they may entirely prevent certain claims or legal challenges from being raised when AI is involved."

And, after providing examples of AI used by the government and AI used by financial planning systems, the researcher offers these sobering thoughts: "All of these problems threaten to leave AI unregulated either because defendants that use AI may never be held liable (e.g., the government's use of AI may prevent a showing of discriminatory intent) or claimants that rely on AI may be left without redress (e.g., because a plaintiff that uses AI to make investment decisions is unable to show reliance)."

A toaster that goes awry will hopefully be a mildly adverse consequence (I can choose to eat the burnt toast or toss it into the trash), while if an AI system that is able to drive a car goes awry, the result can be catastrophic.

Using AI for the driving of cars is a life-or-death instance of AI that is emerging for use in our daily lives.

When you see a car going down the street and there isn't a human driver at the wheel, you are tacitly accepting the belief that the AI is able to drive the car and will not suddenly veer into a crowd of pedestrians or plow into a car ahead of it.

You might counter-argue that the same can said of human drivers, whereby when a human driver is at the wheel, you likewise are accepting the belief that the human will not suddenly ram into pedestrians or into other cars.

If the human did so, we'd all be quickly looking for intent.

Can we do the same for AI driving systems in terms of the actions that they undertake, and does it make sense to even try to ascertain such AI-based intent?

Today's question then is this: *As an example of AI and intent, do we expect AI-based true self-driving cars to embody intention and if so, what does it consist of and how would we know that it exists?*

Let's unpack the matter and see.

The Levels Of Self-Driving Cars

True self-driving cars are ones that the AI drives the car entirely on its own and there isn't any human assistance during the driving task.

These driverless vehicles are considered a Level 4 and Level 5, while a car that requires a human driver to co-share the driving effort is usually considered at a Level 2 or Level 3. The cars that co-share the driving task are described as being semi-autonomous, and typically contain a variety of automated add-on's that are referred to as ADAS (Advanced Driver-Assistance Systems).

There is not yet a true self-driving car at Level 5, which we don't yet even know if this will be possible to achieve, and nor how long it will take to get there.

Meanwhile, the Level 4 efforts are gradually trying to get some traction by undergoing very narrow and selective public roadway trials, though there is controversy over whether this testing should be allowed per se (we are all life-or-death guinea pigs in an experiment taking place on our highways and byways, some point out).

Since semi-autonomous cars require a human driver, the adoption of those types of cars won't be markedly different than driving conventional vehicles, so there's not much new per se to cover about them on this topic (though, as you'll see in a moment, the points next made are generally applicable).

For semi-autonomous cars, it is important that the public needs to be forewarned about a disturbing aspect that's been arising lately, namely that in spite of those human drivers that keep posting videos of themselves falling asleep at the wheel of a Level 2 or Level 3 car, we all need to avoid being misled into believing that the driver can take away their attention from the driving task while driving a semi-autonomous car.

You are the responsible party for the driving actions of the vehicle, regardless of how much automation might be tossed into a Level 2 or Level 3.

Self-Driving Cars And AI Intent

For Level 4 and Level 5 true self-driving vehicles, there won't be a human driver involved in the driving task.

All occupants will be passengers.

The AI is doing the driving.

Let's return to the discussion about intent.

Is the AI that can perform self-driving the same as a toaster?

Intuitively, we might right away proffer that the AI is not at all like a toaster and that making such a callous suggestion undercuts what the AI is accomplishing in being able to drive a car.

Before we dig further into this aspect, I'd like to set the record straight about the AI that is able to drive a car.

Some assume that the AI needed to drive a car must be sentient, able to "think" and perform mental processing on an equivalent basis of humans. So far, that's not the case, and it seems that we'll be able to have AI-based self-driving cars without crossing over into the vaunted singularity (the singularity is considered the moment or occurrence of having AI that transforms from being everyday computational and becoming sentient, having the same unspecified and ill-understood spark that mankind seems to have).

For the moment, remove sentience from this discussion as to the capabilities of AI, and assume that the AI being depicted is computer-based and has not yet achieved human-like equivalency of intelligence. If AI does someday arrive at the singularity, presumably we would need to have an altogether new dialogue about intent, since at that point the AI would be apparently the "same" as human intelligence in one manner or another and the role of intent in its actions would rightfully come onto the table, for sure.

Consider then these forms of intent:
1. **Inscrutable Intent**
2. **Explicated Intent**
3. **AI Developer Intent**
4. **Inserted Intent**
5. **Induced Intent**
6. **Emergent Intent**

Let's start with the notion of inscrutable intent.

It could be that the AI system has an intent and yet we have no means to figure out what the intent is.

For example, the use of Machine Learning (ML) and Deep Learning (DL) oftentimes uses large-scale artificial neural networks (ANNs), which are essentially computer-based simulations of somewhat along the lines of what we believe brains do, though the ML/DL of today is extremely simplistic in comparison and not at all akin to the complexities of the human brain.

In any case, the ML/DL is essentially a mathematical model that is computationally being performed, out of which there is not necessarily any logical basis to explain the inner workings. There are just calculations and arithmetic's taking place. As such, it is generally considered "inscrutable" if there is no ready means to translate this into something meaningful in words and sentences that would constitute an articulated indication of intent.

Next, consider explicated intent.

Some believe that we might be able to do a type of translation of what is happening inside the AI system, and as such, there is a rising call for XAI, known as explainable AI. This is AI that in one fashion or another has been designed and developed to provide an explanation for what it is doing, and thus one might say that could showcase explicated intent.

Many argue that you can just drop the whole worry about AI intention and look instead at the AI developer that crafted the AI.

Since AI is a human-created effort, the human or humans that put it together are the intenders, and therefore the intention of the AI is found within the intentions of those humans.

The difficulty with this human-only as intention source is that the human developer might have crafted AI that goes beyond what the AI developer had in mind.

What do we do when the AI morphs in some manner and no longer abides by what the original human developers intended?

You could argue that no matter what the AI does or becomes, the human developers are still responsible and thus they cannot escape the intention hunt simply by raising their arms and protesting that the AI went beyond their intended aims.

This takes us to the next form of intent, inserted intent.

Essentially, when AI developers craft an AI system, there is an embodiment of "intent" into the computational encoding.

When writing code in say Python or Java or LISP, you could reasonably make the case that the code itself is a reflection of the intent that the human had in their mind. Likewise, even with ML/DL, you could argue that the nature of how the ANN's are set up and trained is a reflection of the intention of the human developers and therefore the structure leaves a kind of trace or residue which reflects intent.

Induced intent consists of the AI itself using the foundational intent that was implanted by the human developers and deriving new intent on top of that cornerstone. I do not want to suggest this is some anthropomorphic amalgamation. More simply stated, the code or underlying structure changes, and as such the presumption of underlying intent changes too.

Finally, the utmost of the induced intent consists of emergent intent, the next level beyond induced, as it were. In the case of emergent intent, the "intent" of the AI becomes relatively far removed from any initial intent that was either inserted or induced and seemingly becomes more semi-independent in appearance.

For AI in self-driving cars, there are critics that point out we do not have as yet any standardized means to identify what the AI intent consists of, other than to resort to asking the AI developers what they did or by trying to scrutinize byzantine code.

I've predicted that once AI self-driving cars become more prevalent, we will begin to see more and more lawsuits that seek redress when an AI self-driving car gets into a car crash or other car incident.

You can readily bet that the notion of intent is going to be raised.

Right now, the matter remains open-ended.

Conclusion

Balderdash, some exhort, there is not anything at all relevant to intent about AI, other than to find out what the humans that developed the AI intended to do.

Maybe so, maybe not.

If you strictly adhere to the assumption that intent is a mental activity or form of mental processing, you could stand on the high ground and assert that AI of today is not akin at all to human mental prowess.

On the other hand, if you are willing to stretch (perhaps quite a bit) the notion of mental processing to encompass the AI systems of today, it does seem to open the door to questions about intent.

For those of you that want to wait to ask questions about AI-intent until the day that sentience and singularity arrive, we can all do so, and let's hope that the AI intentions once that happens are benevolent ones, rather than an intention to squash humans like a bug.

I sleep at night by the snug assumption that such AI will be intending to help and support mankind, and thus human-derived intentions of that indispensable and uplifting spirit will hopefully carry over and be imprinted into the AI itself.

Let's hope so.

.

.

CHAPTER 4

"LIFE ON WHEELS" FILM
AND
AI SELF-DRIVING CARS

CHAPTER 4
"LIFE ON WHEELS" FILM
AND
AI SELF-DRIVING CARS

A timely new film entitled "Life On Wheels" is available online and provides a fast-paced, easy-to-view, and thought-provoking analysis of the mobility revolution that is underway and for which we all need to be giving considerable focus.

Here's the link to the website set up for the film project: https://www.life-onwheels.com/

To watch the film, use the webpage at https://www.life-onwheels.com/distribution and you'll find a link to Amazon where the video is available for viewing (the video is available for free viewing by Amazon Prime members).

Put together by the director/producer seasoned duo of David Hodge and Hi-Jin Kang Hodge, they know how to tell a story that offers a human quality to what otherwise can sometimes be a dry rendition about the ailments of our existing transportation systems.

Using quick video cuts, coupled with shrewdly chosen experts that offer memorable quips and insights about the mobility chores of today and the possible options of greater innovative mobility in the future, this content-packed video clocks in at just a tad less than an hour in length.

By keeping the film to under an hour in viewing time, most that might be interested in a bite-sized learning experience about how our cities and roadway infrastructure crimp us and how we might manage to extricate ourselves from the sordid mess will be suitably placated and satiated.

Though, do realize that the thorny questions raised will have a (hopefully) long-lasting effect on viewers, potentially spurring them to find out how they can partake in their local mobility efforts. It takes a village to establish and maintain a sensible network of mobility options and you might find yourself sparked into action.

Timeliness In Many Ways

In some ways, the film's release is ironically fortuitously aligned with the shelter-in-place efforts taking place around the globe.

How so?

Well, I have witnessed neighbors of mine that for the first time have suddenly seen what has otherwise been hiding in plain sight, namely the sour and sorrowful state of mobility that they are immersed within.

For example, by walking throughout our neighborhood, they have encountered crosswalks that are poorly marked and quite dangerous for those that are not especially attentive. They have discovered that many of our nearby parks are using as much space for the parking of cars as is the space available for wandering amongst greenery (currently, the parking lots are empty, due to the requirement that cars be used only for essential purposes like getting food or going to the doctor, and therefore the conspicuousness of the vast asphalt lots are momentarily visible and no longer surreptitiously hidden by flanks of automobiles).

By and large, the current situation has forced many of us into becoming an everyday type of pedestrian.

Gasp, being a pedestrian, ugh, rather than a driver.

We seem to hold driving in much higher regard socially.

But then came the shelter-in-place or staying-at-home proclamations. As such, we have each now had an unexpected disruption in our usual existence and have by decree gotten outside of the sheltered cocoon of our spiffy cars, awakened anew to the realities of what it is like to try and walk in our suburban streets and along with our city blocks.

As rightfully pointed out in the film, humans seem to have an innate craving for speed, which has motivated us to keenly crave and buy cars, enabling us to drive hurriedly to wherever we might wish to go, despite the fact that walking might be a viable alternative, offering a healthier approach and one that allows our minds to gain contemplative time for indispensable reflective thought.

The high volume of car traffic and agonizingly frustrating roadway congestion that we normally endure is inarguably bad for our physical state, reducing the amount of exercise that we get, and likely untoward for our mental state as we remain glued to the steering wheel and do whatever we can to keep from getting into a car crash.

Speaking of car crashes, the opening scene (trigger alert) showcases the aftermath of what can happen after an automotive incident, sparing us the graphic details, but using the voices of those that are touched by such calamities to express what we typically keep deeply submerged in the backs of our minds.

In short, each time that you get on the road in a car, it is a gigantic contest of death-defying roulette and you never know when that ominous life-or-death gambling wheel is going to sadly halt on your number (this is a number you decidedly don't want to land on).

Of course, our life on wheels does not only have to consist of cars.

The film showcases the rise of scooters and the seeming rebirth of using our bicycles, all of which won't continue unless we ensure that the roadway and the design of our cities are compatible with such ventures.

Cars get the first-class treatment, while everything else seems to get the second-class castoff.

Should we turn that around?

Can we turn it around?

Furthermore, with the emergence of true self-driving or autonomous cars and other such AI-driven vehicles, perhaps we ought to rethink the fundamental design of our cities and our road spaces for a newer age.

Conclusion

In one of my prior articles, I described a famous allegory known as the Upstream Parable (see the **link here)** and indicated how it merits attention in the coming struggle over what mobility is going to be for our future and the future of our children.

The upshot is that we oftentimes are so focused on the downstream activities that we are unable or unaware of looking upstream where the root of the problems might exist.

Via "Life On Wheels" you might be startled into putting your eyes toward the foundational aspects of whether we need to reshape and revamp the structure of our metropolises. Rather than trying to relentlessly and in a perhaps futile manner keep patching what has already been established, it might be time to give walking a new chance at life, and breath fresh air into the intrinsic fact that we are inescapably fashioned by nature as walking animals.

Maybe, just maybe, we can shift our gaze from being auto-centric and instead take stock of being human-centric, creating places where we live, work, play, and share in a more mobility-sensible way, streamlined and committed to being humans and living amongst our fellow humanity.

So, thanks goes to the team that has put together such a perceptive video that vividly depicts how our lives are inextricably intertwined with the miracle of wheels, and asks us pointedly, unabashedly, to seriously rethink the futurescape of transportation and undeniably our very existence.

.

.

CHAPTER 5
MURDER HORNET SPREAD
AND
AI SELF-DRIVING CARS

CHAPTER 5

MURDER HORNET SPREAD AND
AI SELF-DRIVING CARS

Recent headlines about a type of hornet referred to as the "murder hornet" have gotten quite a lot of buzz this past week or so.

It seems that the customary headline-grabbing killer bee is now being overshadowed by a murdering hornet.

Perhaps those forsaken killer bees need a new agent.

Here is a sampling of the hornet mania-inspiring captions:
- The Arrival of the 'Murder Hornet' (*New York Times*)
- 'Murder Hornet' Spotted In The United States (*CBS News*)
- Traps For 'Murder Hornets" Are Being Placed In Tennessee (*Knox News*)

Meanwhile, here are some alternative banners that seem to offer another side about this bespoken and menacingly cutthroat hornet that has come upon us:
- Insect Experts Say People Should Calm Down About The Threat Of 'Murder Hornets' (*Time magazine*)
- Experts Say That 'Murder Hornets' Are Not, In Fact, Invading The US (*Business Insider*)
- Bug Experts Dismiss Worry About US 'Murder Hornets' As Hype (*AP News*)

And in case you are staying awake at night, worrying yourself sick about the invading murderous hornets, this headline might help you get some sleep:

- Praying Mantises Will Save Us All From 'Murder Hornets' (*CNET*)

A superhero apparently awaits in the wings, ready to put a halt to the demented hornets.

But let's take a moment to first figure out what the real story is about these seemingly and unabashedly notorious hornets.

Properly known as the *Vespa mandarinia*, this inch-and-a-half mega-sized hornet is considered a non-native species of the United States (they normally reside in Eastern Asia), and some of them in the Fall of 2019 were able to somehow "invade" into Vancouver Island, Canada, and also ended-up across the border into Washington state.

Efforts have been undertaken by wildlife entomologists and related specialists to find the hornet intruders and attempt to eradicate them.

According to the National Wildlife Federation, there have been no verified reports of the species in this year of 2020 as being spotted in the United States, and "there is currently no cause to believe that any of these hornets are still present in Canada or the U.S." (per a May 8, 2020 posting by the NWF).

Those murdering hornets might be sneaky and perhaps don a disguise, so don't entirely let down your guard, one presupposes.

The nicknamed attribute of "murder" is certainly eye-catching, and unfortunately also simultaneously misleading.

You would be mistaken to think that these dastardly hornets are trying to murder humans, which though this does rarely occur and their sting and bite can be horrifically painful, the real meaning of their murderous nature is that they relish killing honeybees.

Yes, those poor innocent honeybees that are focused on making, well, delicious honey, they are threatened by the murdering hornets that crawl into the honeybee hive and (trigger alert) literally rip the heads off of the beguiled bees, doing so with wild and determined abandon.

If the murdering hornets could establish a foothold in the United States, some say that they could cripple the estimated $15 billion sized economic contributions of honeybees by pretty much wiping out a significant portion of these honey-making creatures. The harmful impact on agriculture would be enormous and a slew of other direct and indirect adverse consequences would arise too.

Protect the honeybees!

Honeybees do have some natural methods to try and repel the attacking hornets, though the U.S. honeybees are not especially versed in doing so since the murdering hornets do not normally reside here. Turns out that the honeybees that have settled in the U.S. are known for their gentleness and not as aggressive toward these invading villainous hornets as comparable bees elsewhere.

In theory, it is possible to genetically try to have us reshape the honeybees, but this carries various risks and complications.

We could use pesticides to try and kill the murdering hornets, but that also has various downsides.

There are some natural predators of the murdering hornets such as the praying mantis, though whether there would be sufficient numbers of the killer of the killers is an open question, plus it might lead to other problems if somehow the praying mantis population suddenly exploded in magnitude.

Besides the threat to the honeybees, there is no doubting the potent punch that this hornet has in its arsenal and its dangers for the American public-at-large.

This wicked hornet has a plentiful volume of venom in its oversized body and can sting repeatedly, proffering a feeling as though you have been harshly stung via an overheated deep-piercing metal pin. In addition, the stinger is said to be so strong and lengthy that it can puncture right through the usual protective gear that beekeepers use for safety purposes.

These voracious hornets are also willing and eager to go after other insects and we would likely see bumblebees getting ravaged too.

All in all, the best bet would be to stop the invader before it establishes a beachhead.

Since the initial foray seems to be in a relatively confined geographical area, the hope is to focus efforts on finding and destroying the hornets there, first and foremost.

At the same time, let's hope that the mania about the murdering hornets doesn't get out-of-hand and leads people into trying to on-their-own kill everyday hornets that are already native to our lands. That wouldn't be good either. And, perhaps equally as bad or worse, it is said that some people have been killing honeybees under the confused mindset that somehow the bees are the problem, rather than the hornets, or that if they kill the bees it will prevent the hornets from coming around (or, some other oddball and completely foolhardy notions).

Anyway, as mentioned, the hysteria will hopefully subside, and meanwhile, the scientists and wildlife specialists will be seeking to detect and prevent the invading hornets from spreading.

That's a laudable goal.

Turns out, there is another inadvertent human-led action that could potentially undermine the efforts to contain and curtail the appalling hornet.

Here's today's intriguing question: *Could the advent of AI-based true self-driving cars unintentionally spread these bad-to-the-bone hornets and perhaps other invasive species?*

Let's unpack the matter and see.

The Levels Of Self-Driving Cars

True self-driving cars are ones that the AI drives the car entirely on its own and there isn't any human assistance during the driving task.

These driverless vehicles are considered a Level 4 and Level 5, while a car that requires a human driver to co-share the driving effort is usually considered at a Level 2 or Level 3. The cars that co-share the driving task are described as being semi-autonomous, and typically contain a variety of automated add-on's that are referred to as ADAS (Advanced Driver-Assistance Systems).

There is not yet a true self-driving car at Level 5, which we don't yet even know if this will be possible to achieve, and nor how long it will take to get there.

Meanwhile, the Level 4 efforts are gradually trying to get some traction by undergoing very narrow and selective public roadway trials, though there is controversy over whether this testing should be allowed per se (we are all life-or-death guinea pigs in an experiment taking place on our highways and byways, some point out).

Since semi-autonomous cars require a human driver, the adoption of those types of cars won't be markedly different than driving conventional vehicles, so there's not much new per se to cover about them on this topic (though, as you'll see in a moment, the points next made are generally applicable).

For semi-autonomous cars, it is important that the public needs to be forewarned about a disturbing aspect that's been arising lately, namely that in spite of those human drivers that keep posting videos of themselves falling asleep at the wheel of a Level 2 or Level 3 car, we all need to avoid being misled into believing that the driver can take away their attention from the driving task while driving a semi-autonomous car.

You are the responsible party for the driving actions of the vehicle, regardless of how much automation might be tossed into a Level 2 or Level 3.

Self-Driving Cars And Spreading Bad Things

For Level 4 and Level 5 true self-driving vehicles, there won't be a human driver involved in the driving task.

All occupants will be passengers.

The AI is doing the driving.

Many believe that the advent of AI-based true self-driving cars will help to significantly reduce the number of annual fatalities and injuries that occur due to car crashes, numbering around 40,000 deaths and approximately 2.3 million injuries in the United States alone each year (see **this link here** for my collection of stats about national and international driving incidents).

In addition, it is hoped that the emergence of self-driving cars will provide mobility for those that today are mobility disadvantaged. There is an ongoing issue in our country about the cost of mobility and the access to mobility, all of which it is predicted will be likely alleviated via the prevalence of true self-driving cars, leading to an era of mobility-for-all.

The bright and rosy picture of a future with self-driving cars is not quite though the full picture.

One downside that needs to be dealt with involves the potential for a massive encroaching upon our personal privacy. This privacy issue involves the very key elements that make conventional cars into becoming true self-driving cars, namely the addition of sensory devices such as cameras, radar, ultrasonic, LIDAR, and other such devices.

Why might those advanced pieces of tech be anything but wholly beneficial?

They have the potential for becoming a Big Brother roving eye.

Think of it this way.

Every time that a car goes down your neighborhood street, imagine that the vehicle was chockful of cameras videotaping whatever is happening on your local street. This video could be uploaded into the cloud via the OTA (Over-The-Air) electronic communications of the self-driving car and be ultimately stitched together with similar data from hundreds, thousands, perhaps hundreds of thousands of other self-driving cars.

In short, our cars become a snitch of our every move.

Who owns that data?

When can that data be used?

We are all going to be involuntarily recorded, doing so without our expressed permission, simply by walking around our streets and roadways, and a vast collection of data can be mined to figure out where you were, where you went, what you looked like, etc.

That is something to be given due thought, and as a society, it provides a somber and serious matter to be wrestled with.

Meanwhile, there are other ways in which the advent of self-driving cars might have drawbacks.

Remember the murdering hornets?

They seem to be currently relegated to a relatively small geographical area, apparently in the northern part of Washington state.

That is certainly handy since it makes things easier to try and find and eradicate them.

Suppose though that the evildoer hornets were able to readily spread across the United States.

Now, you might argue that they could eventually do so, on their own, mile by mile, state by state, which is indeed the case, but the odds are that it would take quite a while for them to undertake such a migration. It would be somewhat slow and perhaps sluggish enough for us to detect them at each step and continue to try and blot them out.

Imagine instead if they were somehow magically able to transport themselves to all parts of the country, rapidly, and without any discernable pattern of expansion.

It would be problematic to try and halt their progress.

This presumed magical carpet ride would provide a perfect means for them to make inroads all across our great country.

And, wait for it, hold your breath, ready yourself, it could be that the magical carpet ride would be the use of true self-driving cars.

Those nasty murdering hornets could try to latch themselves onto a car, let's say via the underbody or under-the-hood, and then go for a freeride, jumping off like a hitchhiker at whatever next locale seemed of interest.

I'm not suggesting that the hornets are astute enough to realize that a car is a car, and nor that a self-driving car is a self-driving car, and only pointing out that by dumb luck the hornets might end-up hitching onto a self-driving car and go along for an easy and wide-ranging trip.

I know that you are already carping that there wouldn't seem to be any difference between the hornets riding on a conventional car versus a self-driving car, and thus, it seems perhaps untoward to single out self-driving cars as an especially unsavory and unawares culprit.

Well, let's include some added factors.

Currently, we drive our conventional cars a relatively short distance, using our endearing vehicles to get to work and home, along with trips to the grocery store or the gym.

Sure, we occasionally go on a summertime road trip, but that's generally a rarer use of our cars and not the bulk of the miles consumed.

Some believe that self-driving cars will radically alter our distance going proclivities.

If you wanted to drive a large distance such as visiting a friend or relatives in a nearby state, you would need to drive that distance and likely take breaks as you do so. You might even need to have at least one other adult driver ready to take the wheel, in case you get sleepy or weary. It's a heck of a chore and one that we tend to avoid doing, today.

Consider instead the use of a true self-driving car.

You are not driving and there isn't any human needed for the driving.

Thus, you get into the self-driving car, tell the AI that you want to go visit your friend or relative, and the rest of the time you can play Parcheesi or binge-watch a favorite show or fall asleep.

The odds are that many models of self-driving cars will be outfitted to allow the seats to recline, allowing you to get a sorely needed nap while undertaking your morning commute to work or for those long road trips that could use a plethora of sleep.

There are even designs of self-driving car interiors that encompass the ability to quickly swivel and click the seats into actual beds. And so on.

In short, the odds are that people will take self-driving cars for much longer trips than they ever imagined undertaking via a conventional human-driven car.

Wait for a second, you say, if that's the case then why aren't more people using buses to get across the country, since it effectively is "driverless" from the perspective of the rider (i.e., yes, there is a human bus driver, though you as the passenger aren't involved with and presumably do not need to be involved in any of the driving itself).

Generally, people are not especially willing to ride in a long-haul bus to get across the country, partially due to the need to schedule the matter and also the obvious requirement to be amongst many other people, while for a self-driving car you just can on-the-spur of the moment hail one, and with relative privacy go on a journey to wherever you want to go.

Some even believe that the use of short-haul flights will decrease by quite a bit since people will choose to use a self-driving car instead. There is the ease of doing so, along with not having to go through the usual security checkpoints at airports and will therefore undoubtedly offer a compelling and alluring alternative to flying.

The point is that the advent of self-driving cars promises to enable us all to go on very long driving trips, as much as we like, and therefore we will begin to see car-related traffic that stretches from coast-to-coast, far beyond what we see today as primarily localized traffic in a relatively confined geographical area.

For the murderous hornets, it's a proverbial leave the driving to us, via our AI, and we'll take you wherever we are going.

That's why I had mentioned earlier the notion that a magic carpet might appear to provide a means for the unwanted hornets to populate across the country, and for which there would not be any specifically identifiable pattern of the migration. The migration would be based on wherever people are going in their self-driving cars.

This would, in turn, be a nightmare for those trying to detect and fight the nefarious hornets.

Aha, some might exclaim, proof that we are embarking upon making our own Frankenstein that will inevitably turn upon ourselves.

Conclusion

Before you start to lose sleep over the idea that self-driving cars are going to be a naive rube and unintended transmitter of the disreputable hornets, we do need to bring reality back into the picture.

We are still a long way from having true self-driving cars.

The number of experimental self-driving cars on our roadways today is a teensy tiny number of cars, and those tryouts are happening in quite confined geographical areas, partially due to the lack of sophistication as yet of the self-driving capabilities (see my discussion about Operational Design Domains or ODDs at **this link here**), and partially as it is more economical right now to do so.

The unwelcomed hornets are going to have to wait quite a while if they wish to use self-driving cars.

Get in line like the rest of us, one might say.

Meanwhile, it is certainly worth contemplating what we might do in the future and whether we will need to be more cognizant of how readily we can spread adverse things from place to place, via the added ease of car travel and the use of self-driving cars.

Furthermore, let's not neglect the self-driving trucks that are being experimented with. Those obviously have as much chance if not more so of allowing for the rapid spread of something, given that they are purposely intended to go across the country, plus they offer a much larger surface or body onto which something could secret a ride.

There is a famous expression about being as mad as a hornet.

We should be careful about letting the genie out of the bottle, as it were, with respect to the advent of AI-based self-driving cars, and not allow ourselves to inadvertently shoot our own foot by providing a new way to spread untoward things around our country.

If we do, I suppose we will all be madder than a hornet.

.

.

CHAPTER 6

SIMONS SIGHT RESEARCH
AND
AI SELF-DRIVING CARS

CHAPTER 6

SIMONS SIGHT RESEARCH
AND
AI SELF-DRIVING CARS

The Simons Institute for the Theory of Computing at the University of California Berkeley is a highly regarded venue that was established in 2012 and has been bringing together computer scientists and other allied experts in an effort to explore deep and unsolved computational problems.

Besides conducting various workshops and symposia, along with publishing research papers, the Simons Institute has recently launched a new online video documentary series.

As an excellent and well-worth watching opener for the video series, the first such video is entitled "Perception as Inference: The Brain and Computation" and is both informative and engaging, offering a vivid and telling exploration of how the eye captures visual images, along with the vital intertwining of the brain and the mind in making sense of what the eye is observing.

It is jam-packed with a quite fascinating and readily explicated background on the topic, mixing together both theory and practice, and offers a riveting style that clocks in at less than 20 minutes, moving along at a unified pace and amazingly covers rather substantive content in such a short timeframe.

Kudos goes to Dr. Bruno Olshausen, Professor in the Helen Wills Neuroscience Institute and the School of Optometry, and with an affiliated appointment in Electrical Engineering and Computer Science (EECS), as he is the expert extraordinaire for this enlightening video about the eye-brain duality.

I'll provide some tidbits from the video, whetting your appetite to view it, and also offer some thoughts on an allied use case involving the advent of Autonomous Vehicles (AV) and especially the emergence of AI-based self-driving cars.

The Eyes As Visual Sensory Devices

We often take our eyes for granted and give little attention to how they work and why they work.

In many respects, it is a kind of biological and neural sensory miracle that our eyes and our brain are able to seamlessly work hand-in-hand, an intertwining of our vision system with our cognitive capabilities that enables us to perceive the world and make sense of what we are viewing (most of the time, one hopes).

As stated in the video, our sense-making of the visual inputs can lead to hallucinations, though as aptly pointed out, one could ingeniously argue that we are perhaps always hallucinating (for some, a startling and yet useful way to understand the matter), and we manage fortunately most of the time to do a prudent job by turning the raw imagery into rational meaning for operating in our day-to-day lives.

If you were to separate the eyes from the brain (ugh, sorry if that seems untoward), you would have essentially a standalone sensory device that is collecting visually stimulated data but that has no place to go, and for which there would not be any viable sense-making in terms of embellishing the data and leveraging the data for comprehension purposes.

This is worth contemplating as there are many that oftentimes make a mistaken or ill-informed analogy to the use of electronic-based cameras and the taking of pictures and the recording of video, and it is important to set the record straight that though you might assert that such cameras are the equivalent of the eye, this tends to egregiously downplay the role of the brain and mind in the essential duality involved.

In short, a camera can provide images that we then as humans can watch and make sense from the visualizations proffered using our brains, but the camera itself is not particularly doing any sense-making per se.

In the use case of AV's and AI-based self-driving cars, you can place cameras onto a car and collect as much visual data as you might seek, yet the ability to make sense of the images, such as determining that there is a pedestrian about to cross the street and might get hit, this comes from the AI side of the computational effort.

We obviously already know how to produce cameras (which do keep improving), while it's another matter altogether to figure out how to process the visual data and turn it into anything nearing the brain's ability to transform visual imagery into cogent thoughts and actions.

That's part of the so-called "hold-up" in the crafting of self-driving cars, namely, how to transform the rudimentary visual data into cognitive-like comprehension that an AI system might embody and translate into then appropriately and safely steering the wheels of the car, along with operating the accelerator and brake pedals.

It is indisputably a hard problem and bodes great challenges.

Another important facet involves the aspect that the eyes are registering visual imagery that inherently contains visual clutter and noise, comprising numerous distortions, and is frequently unstable and non-uniformly being sampled, etc.

Simply stated, the visual imagery is not at all pristine and the neural processing has to overcome and transform this raw input accordingly.

You could liken this somewhat to the data provided by the cameras on a self-driving car.

Imagine that a self-driving car is rocketing down the freeway in the rain. The video data that is streaming into the sensors is partially occluded and altered too amidst the jostling and motion of the vehicle, being chockful of various noisiness and distortions, all of which the AI-based driving system must try to screen and computationally analyze.

Human drivers are generally able to drive a car and do so primarily via the sensing of the road and the use of their eyes, seemingly effortlessly and with little awareness of their eye-mind dual processing at play.

Attempts to replicate this kind of human-led activity by the use of cameras and AI-processing in self-driving vehicles are making rudimentary progress, though much remains to be solved.

Humans, of course, have two eyes, though my parents always seemed to have a third eye in the back of their heads, while the Jumping Spider has 8 eyes and the Box Jellyfish has an astounding 24 eyes.

Presumably, in a Darwinian fashion, creatures on this planet have evolved toward some befitting number and style of eyes that align with their environment and their base survival.

In the case of self-driving cars, there are arguments aplenty regarding how many cameras and the type of cameras that should best be used to achieve true self-driving.

Furthermore, there are ongoing acrimonious debates about whether other sensory devices such as radar and LIDAR should be used, which some suggest that since humans don't have such innate capabilities as radar and LIDAR, perhaps self-driving should be done entirely via cameras and not require such additional sensory elements.

There are also many computationally inspired debates on these AV topics.

For example, the human eye and the brain seem to be operating on a basis that one could apply Bayesian inference (quite well-explained in the video), and as such this same modeling technique might be used for the AI processing in self-driving cars.

Some though are uncomfortable with the incorporating of probabilistic based computations into AI driving systems and believe that somehow the AI needs to deal in only absolute certainties, a seemingly incongruous notion when compared to the realities of driving.

Conclusion

By deftly crafting increasingly sophisticated computational models of the eye and the eye-brain duality, we can attempt to emulate the actions of this miracle of nature and dramatically improve our computer-based mechanizations accordingly.

Meanwhile, such modeling is indubitably and inexorably going to teasingly reveal the deep dark secrets underlying this remarkable wetware and get us stepwise closer to one day cracking their enigmatic code.

This first video in the Simons Institute series is a go-getter that out-the-gate provides an invigorating look at a crucial slice of perception and addresses numerous computational aspects that are bound to get you thinking.

Keep your eyes open and be on the watch for more such videos.

Your eye-mind duality will thank you for doing so.

.

CHAPTER 7
NASCAR CAR RACING
AND
AI SELF-DRIVING CARS

CHAPTER 7

NASCAR CAR RACING

AND

AI SELF-DRIVING CARS

"Drivers, start your engines" was the battle cry this weekend.

NASCAR racing is back underway after a ten-week halt due to the pandemic, and Sunday's winner was long-time race car driver Kevin Harvick, also known as *The Closer* or *Happy Harvick*.

He certainly did the closing on Sunday and indubitably seemed quite happy with the outcome.

There were forty race cars and each of the 40 drivers expressed elation to be racing once again after the lengthy furlough. Just behind Harvick came Alex Bowman, Kurt Busch, Chase Elliot, and Denny Hamlin, rounding out the top five finishers.

Besides eager and faithful fans watching online (broadcast via Fox), there were plenty of new fans that opted to tune-in since this was one of the first professional sporting events to take place as the post-pandemic new-normal starts to emerge.

And it was generally a normal NASCAR race, encompassing spin-outs, car wrecks including one that happened within the first 15 seconds of the start, cars bumping into each other with sweet kisses, wall scrapings of ear screeching delight, and pretty much the usual fanfare, though there weren't any fans in the stands at the event itself.

You could readily discern that each of the drivers was there to compete, fiercely so, as usual, and the traditional showmanship and jockeying for position was evident throughout the entire race.

Of course, each driver has their own driving style and brings to the race an individualized perspective on how to best drive their car and how to presumably succeed at winning the race.

Though they are all different in their backgrounds and experiences, they do have one thing indisputably in common, namely, they are all humans.

Say what?

Yes, the NASCAR drivers of today are human beings.

The reason that I point out that they are members of humanity is that this kind of car race will someday likely include AI-based true self-driving cars.

In that case, there will be AI drivers, ones of the artificial variety.

This won't mean that there will be robots sitting in the driver's seat of the race cars. Instead, the AI system is essentially under-the-hood, or more likely running on souped-up computer processors that are placed carefully inside the car and stationed away from the heat of the engine and protected from the car bashings that sometimes occur.

It will certainly seem eerie to see NASCAR cars that are completely empty and absent of a human driver as those revved up vehicles scoot around the track.

One small point of clarification, there isn't any reason that we won't eventually have robots that are car drivers, it's just that for now, the most expedient way to develop AI self-driving cars is via on-board computers rather than using a robot.

There is no doubt that making a robot that could walk and talk, along with being able to drive a car would be a huge benefit to society. Part of the benefit is that such a robot could drive any conventional car, and we, therefore, would not need to replace existing cars with newer and more expensive ones that are jampacked with sensors and computers.

Anyway, do not hold your breath waiting for the robots that drive, but go ahead and place it on something to see one day as part of your revered bucket list.

My basis for bringing up the notion of self-driving cars being in the NASCAR race was prompted during the weekend while watching the event via Zoom and with several beer-drinking friends. They wanted to know what the race would be like if there were self-driving cars included.

That is a great question and worthy of some serious noodling.

Today's intriguing question then is this: *Will AI-based true self-driving cars compete in car races such as NASCAR and if so, what will the results be?*

Let's unpack the matter and see.

The Levels Of Self-Driving Cars

True self-driving cars are ones that the AI drives the car entirely on its own and there isn't any human assistance during the driving task.

These driverless vehicles are considered a Level 4 and Level 5, while a car that requires a human driver to co-share the driving effort is usually considered at a Level 2 or Level 3.

The cars that co-share the driving task are described as being semi-autonomous, and typically contain a variety of automated add-on's that are referred to as ADAS (Advanced Driver-Assistance Systems).

There is not yet a true self-driving car at Level 5, which we don't yet even know if this will be possible to achieve, and nor how long it will take to get there.

Meanwhile, the Level 4 efforts are gradually trying to get some traction by undergoing very narrow and selective public roadway trials, though there is controversy over whether this testing should be allowed per se (we are all life-or-death guinea pigs in an experiment taking place on our highways and byways, some point out).

Since semi-autonomous cars require a human driver, the adoption of those types of cars won't be markedly different than driving conventional vehicles, so there's not much new per se to cover about them on this topic (though, as you'll see in a moment, the points next made are generally applicable).

For semi-autonomous cars, it is important that the public needs to be forewarned about a disturbing aspect that's been arising lately, namely that in spite of those human drivers that keep posting videos of themselves falling asleep at the wheel of a Level 2 or Level 3 car, we all need to avoid being misled into believing that the driver can take away their attention from the driving task while driving a semi-autonomous car.

You are the responsible party for the driving actions of the vehicle, regardless of how much automation might be tossed into a Level 2 or Level 3.

Self-Driving Cars And Car Racing

For Level 4 and Level 5 true self-driving vehicles, there won't be a human driver involved in the driving task.

All occupants will be passengers.

The AI is doing the driving.

Let's consider how car racing will be altered as a result of including AI true self-driving cars.

One of the foremost questions to consider is whether AI-driven cars will be competing with human-driven cars, or perhaps the two will be kept separate from each other.

In other words, we all might decide that it is best to have AI compete against AI, and humans compete against humans, and neither the twain shall meet.

Though that might be a chosen approach, I doubt that we would all be satisfied with such an arrangement. Just as we love watching AI compete against the top chess players, it would seem a natural form of human curiosity to witness AI competing against human race-car drivers.

So, we can reasonably assume that there will be car races involving both AI-driven cars and human-driven cars.

Okay, in that case, who will win?

You might immediately exclaim that such a race is uneven and unfair, and that the AI would certainly whip the human drivers and readily outdrive them.

If you say such a thing, I believe you have been watching too many science fiction movies and seen plenty of similar plots on TV shows.

The answer today is that it would be a toss-up as to whether the AI would win or the human drivers would win.

In short, you could expect as much excitement in the race as you would if it were entirely humans driving the cars.

Why so, you might be wondering and perhaps puzzled or perplexed about the matter.

It would seem that the AI ought to be able to precisely drive and do so without any of the usual human foibles involved in driving. The steely-eyed AI would lack emotions. It would not get tired. It would not get upset when another driver shoved its vehicle out of the way to make an end-around.

For everyday driving on our neighborhood streets and our vaunted freeways, it is indeed assumed and hoped that the AI self-driving cars will do away with the 40,000 fatalities each year in the United States due to existing car crashes and likewise reduce the 2.3 million injuries that occur. The AI system will not drive while intoxicated, and it will not be distracted while driving, all of which is undertaken by human drivers and leads sadly to those otherwise avoidable deaths and injuries.

But driving on a racetrack is a different story.

Realize that a racetrack is a set-aside place for driving.

There aren't pedestrians that can wander into the middle of the lanes. The lanes themselves are well-marked and the roadway is in pristine condition. There are stated rules about driving behaviors and how the race will be conducted.

One good aspect of this constrained environment is that it does lessen the effort by the AI since it will not need to scan for bike riders or wayward jaywalkers. This is a heads-down and keenly focused effort to race a car.

The human racecar drivers are there for the same reasons and under the same conditions.

Thus, whether AI or human, the driver is attempting to maximize the speed and control of the car, aiming to outgun and outlast the other vehicles in the competition.

For today's efforts underway to craft self-driving cars, there isn't much interest in car racing, which won't bring in the big bucks by having developed and fielded self-driving cars. As such, there is pretty much only experimental work about pushing AI to the limits of the vehicle dynamics (see my coverage on that topic at **this link here**).

By and large, the AI driving systems right now would not be as astute at driving a race car as would a seasoned race car driver like those in the NASCAR race.

In addition, winning a topnotch car race is not simply about the use of the driving controls.

Racecar drivers need to use their wits too.

They must gauge how their fellow drivers are driving. In a split second, decisions need to be made about whether to try and browbeat another driver or whether to fade back and let them push forward.

This is a chess match on wheels, involving efforts to out psyche your opponents and outmaneuver them.

Though I am sure that race car drivers and race car fans will adore the comparison to chess, I do want to gently mention that some would argue that the strategies in driving are not quite the same as the strategies involved in chess, and thus just as chess doesn't require as much physical dexterity as does car racing, it could be said that car racing doesn't require the same levels of mental adroitness as does chess (I suppose those are fighting words, sorry about that).

The overarching point is that an AI system that can drive a car for purposes of getting you from your home to the grocery is not the same AI that is going to win a heralded car race.

When I earlier mentioned Level 4 and Level 5 self-driving cars, one salient aspect that now comes to play here is that the Level 4 self-driving cars are considered drivable within a defined Operational Design Domain (ODD).

One such ODD might be that the AI system is able to drive in Phoenix, on days that are not rainy, and only during daylight hours. Thus, an ODD usually specifies the geographical constraints, the time and roadway conditions, and other particulars that involve the limitations of the AI driving capability.

In theory, a self-driving car that would be entered into a first-rate race would need to have been crafted to abide by an ODD that befits the car racing realm.

These are being worked on, and we'll need to see how well they can perform.

Pitting Persons Versus Machines

Suppose that such an AI self-driving car was ready to enter into a NASCAR race.

What then?

Well, even in that case, the AI is still not a hands-down winner.

During car races, there is a lot of uncertainty that arises.

Racecar drivers will tell you that a patch of an oil slick can ruin your day while driving at high speeds and on tight turns.

Your car tires during the race will suffer wear-and-tear and their performance when rounding turns are not utterly guaranteed.

Even if an AI system is driving at a race car level, the AI is still subject to the physics of the car, and the physics and conditions of the track, all of which can undermine the AI driving system as it attempts to compete in the race.

The randomness of the physical elements will be a factor in dashing the efforts of the AI, just as it would for those living and breathing human race car drivers.

Speaking of which, there is another quite significant factor that needs to be entered into these calculations.

Those darned human drivers.

They add a lot of uncertainty into the race too.

Will that human car driver let the AI-driven car go past, or will the human driver stand their ground?

This brings up another salient point about AI driving systems.

Currently, one of the qualms expressed about the day-to-day AI driving systems is that they are docile and drive like a skittish newbie behind the wheel. Human drivers that know this are frequently taking advantage of the AI self-driving cars, doing so by purposely cutting in front of the self-driving car or making threatening micro-motions of their human-driven car to get the self-driving car to let them slip past.

At four-way stop signs, there have been instances of self-driving cars that come to a full stop, legally abiding by the laws, and meanwhile human drivers arrive at the stop sign and do rolling stops. The AI system waits patiently for those other human drivers to proceed ahead. Those pesky humans will take advantage of this propensity and the AI self-driving car might sit there for minutes at a time, waiting until those human drivers allow the self-driving car to proceed.

There seems to be little courtesy extended from human drivers toward AI drivers.

If that's the case, should we expect the AI driving systems to become more aggressive?

Some argue that yes, we must do so. The AI must be as selfish and greedy as are human drivers if it is going to be amidst human drivers in daily traffic, those proponents say.

This brings us back to the car racing matter.

I think we can all agree that an AI driving system that is relatively docile is not going to beat the NASCAR human drivers during a race.

Those humans would clean the clock of the AI.

Easy-peasy, you might point out, just make the AI into an aggressive race car driver.

Yes, but how far do we go, and might this ratchet up the dangers for the human race car drivers. Sure, they are already endangered by their fellow human drivers, but there is an honor code or esprit de corps that to some extent moderates how far they can push the boundaries. It will be hard to tune the AI to just the right balance of aggressiveness versus killer attitude.

Conclusion

For those race car drivers that are fearful of the day that AI self-driving cars enter into the ring with them, they can somewhat rest easy for the moment.

For safety purposes, the odds are that the AI self-driving cars would first be pitted against their fellow AI self-driving cars.

Once that is somewhat played out, there will be some gingerly probing efforts to have AI self-driving cars race against human race car drivers.

Think about how many fans this would undoubtedly bring to the race car driving realm.

Everyone would want to see how well the battle of mankind versus the machine will go. Bets would most likely be on both sides of the equation, with some absolutely sure the AI would prevail, while others convinced that the human race car driver has no equal among AI.

Now, here's a bit of a twist.

Suppose that the AI systems communicated with each other during the race, ganging up on the human race car drivers.

You know how sneaky AI can be.

Would the human race car drivers be willing to align among themselves to beat the AI self-driving cars, or would those human drivers be so focused on each person or thing for themselves that the AI could leverage its willingness to form an AI clique and outmatch the humans on a divide-and-conquer basis?

Taking this a step further, imagine if the AI were to suddenly reach the so-called singularity during a car race, which is considered the moment that AI is going to flip over into being sentient. At that vaunted point, the AI would be seemingly considered to have the same "being" status as do humans, and quite a miracle if it indeed happened.

I'm not sure that we would care at that moment as to who wins the car race, and instead, we'd be trying to see whether the AI is going to be peaceful and coexist with humans or perhaps take a different tack and try to wipe us out.

Say, maybe it would be best if the human drivers at that moment let the AI win, doing so as a gesture exhibiting the kindness and magnanimity of humanity.

NASCAR, did you hear that?

CHAPTER 8

BALLOT HARVESTING
AND
AI SELF-DRIVING CARS

CHAPTER 8

BALLOT HARVESTING

AND

AI SELF-DRIVING CARS

There is a lot of controversy about ballot harvesting.

First, some prefer to call it ballot collecting, since the word "harvesting" seems ominous and suggests a foul act.

Others insist that due to the potential for the underhanded activity that might occur when performing ballot collecting that the effort genuinely deserves to have the harvesting moniker.

In general, the notion is that people provided with vote-by-mail paper-based voting that enables them to vote from their homes are susceptible to all sorts of chicanery, and as such this undermines the legitimacy of the voting process.

And if the voting process is perceived as untoward it then mars the outcome of elections, which might be based on the perception of how the voting occurred or might also entail actual voting irregularities.

What kind of voting irregularities might arise?

Some assert that there are rampant chances of fraudulent voting, some of which would be clearly considered illegal, while other acts might be borderline in their deceptive nature or have an appalling stench of illegality.

For example, a voter's mail-in ballot arrives in their mailbox and someone grabs it from the mail receptacle and proceeds to fill it in, then signs it, and either mails it or opts to carry it to a ballot submission center. Thus, in this case, the intended voter never actually saw the ballot and the interloper is masquerading as that voter.

There seems little doubt that such an act is a form of fraudulent voting.

Consider next the case of a voter receiving their ballot via mail and perhaps otherwise not necessarily intending to make use of it. Suppose that someone comes to their door and indicates they are there to pick-up the ballot, seemingly as though doing so in an official or semi-official manner. The voter might be confused or unsure of what to do, and hands over the blank ballot. The receiver then proceeds as per the prior use case and completes the ballot and submits it.

Once again, the true voter was not the actual voter, and this too is pretty clearly a fraudulent act.

Getting into shades of gray, suppose the door ringer explains that they can help the voter with the filling out of the ballot, and proceeds to sit with the voter in doing so. Step by step, this "helper" shows the voter which places to mark their votes, including who they should vote for. The voter might perceive this as valued assistance since perhaps they had little idea of what votes to cast and were also intimidated by the ballot form and hesitant to try and fill it out on their own.

The "helper" then has the voter sign the ballot and offers to make sure it will get delivered.

Is this a fraudulent act?

Assuming that the voter filled in the form and signed it without any apparent coercion, this instance is likely permitted, though there is a small twist on the aspect of proceeding to deliver the completed ballot.

In some states, such ballots are only to be turned-in by a family member, thus the "helper" might be performing an illegal act in the delivery of the ballot, assuming they were not a family member.

Some states allow that the ballot delivery can be done by anyone in the household of the voter, in addition to the possibility of being a family member. This means that if Joe, a non-family member of Jane, and yet living in the same household as Jane, he could legally deliver the ballot to a receiving center. Or, in some states, the other person could be a caregiver and not necessarily living in the household at all.

Other states allow that essentially anyone can act for a voter in terms of delivering their completed ballot. In that sense, the "helper" could be an utter stranger that perchance came to the door and sought the ballot from the voter.

Such "helpers" can collect just one or a few such ballots or might be legally able to collect dozens or even an unlimited number, depending upon the state laws covering the act.

There are more variants involved in this process.

Suppose the "helper" watches quietly while the voter marks the ballot and signs it, and then offers to deliver the ballot for the voter. Upon going out the door of the home, the "helper" then proceeds to change the voter indicated markings, opting to vote for someone other than whom the voter intended.

That's a no-no.

Or, suppose the voter did not sign the ballot, perhaps being told by the "helper" that there is no need to do so, and in fact, the voter was reluctant to sign it because (suppose) some of the votes marked weren't what the voter preferred (but the voter was led to those markings by the interloper). After departing with the unsigned ballot, the interloper then signs it, attempting to forge the signature of the voter.

Another big no-no.

One of the concerns underlying this whole aspect of ballot collecting is that there is a risk that the aforementioned deviousness and at times illegal voting can take place.

This risk is presumably increased due to the role of money and politics.

The alleged "helper" might have been paid to come and collect the ballot from someone's home. On the one hand, you could claim this is a handy service to aid the collecting of ballots. At the same time, this might be an incentive for the "helper" to intentionally get ballots completed, perhaps due to getting paid by the number of ballots collected.

You might think that it doesn't matter if the "helper" is being paid to collect the ballot, as long as they merely collect it and do not otherwise interfere or interject themselves into the voting act itself. Of course, there are some that argue that with money on the line, it is overly tempting to cross that line and exceed the proper boundaries in order to get a collectible ballot and thus earn the dough.

In some states, these "helper" collectors cannot be paid by the number of ballots and instead can only be paid by the hour. The thinking is that this reduces the incentive to cross the line when collecting ballots, though others argue that this is still a ruse and that any payment is tantamount to encouraging improper acts.

Meanwhile, others insist that these "helpers" are aiding the voters by inspiring them to cast their votes, urging them on via offering to collect and deliver ballots. Presumably, we want as many legitimate voters to readily be able to cast their votes as possible, and anything that reduces the friction associated with voting is touted as contributory to our democracy.

There are slippery slopes that raise eyebrows and seem emboldened by these practices, some point out.

Suppose the being-paid "helper" offers to split some of the money with the voter, providing an added incentive to the voter to cast a vote. Or, the "helper" intimidates or threatens the voter to fill-in and sign the ballot, presumably doing so as a desire to get the money by having another ballot to deliver.

Those kinds of acts are certainly considered illegal if proven to have occurred, though the question arises as to how it would be discovered that such acts took place, and thus, they might go undetected or ultimately unreconciled.

It lurks in the murky background and can cloud the integrity of the votes and the election results.

You can take out the money element and substitute a political motive instead. If the "helper" is politically motivated to carry out such acts, regardless of any direct payment, some worry that these ilks will occur, nonetheless.

Trying to gauge how much of this actually happens has been problematic, and likewise predicting how much it will happen going forward is equally problematic.

Indisputably, it is a whopping colossal mess.

The vote-by-mail topic continues to be a polarizing issue and spurs heated debates in many respects, including though not solely due to the ballot collecting or ballot harvesting matter (there are additional qualms about mailed ballots).

Should we dispense with vote-by-mail, some ask?

It is a necessity, some emphasize, and the use of vote-by-mail is essential since there are voters that cannot otherwise get to a voting place. Perhaps they are mobility disadvantaged and have no ready means to travel to a polling place. The vote-by-mail provision provides them an opportunity to exercise their right to vote, which otherwise might languish simply as a result of the location of where they were otherwise supposed to cast their vote.

Plus, with the pandemic and its possible aftermath, there are worries that going to polling places might be unhealthful and therefore serves as a further prompter for allowing and potentially expanding vote-by-mail capabilities.

Could though an increase in vote-by-mail lead to an increase in the various interloper deceptive schemes and possibly spark even more angst about the legitimacy of the votes?

Some believe that it would, arguing passionately that any all-told benefits of the vote-by-mail approach are unquestionably outweighed by its negatives. Others just as fervently believe that it would not delegitimize the voting and insist that the benefits indisputably outweigh the actual or perceived negative consequences.

Shifting gears, technologists are apt to find the entire topic somewhat exasperating as they would likely point out that we ought to go completely online for voting in elections.

Forget about those paper-based ballots and the archaic use of snail mail, or other kinds of physical delivery of one means or another, and just go modern and do all voting online.

You could even do away with polling places, though it is conceded that they could still exist if the cost and desire to do so was still existent.

We probably will inevitably end up in an online voting world, though getting there is likely to be more arduous and controversial than you might at first assume.

A typical qualm includes the possibility that an online voter is not the actual voter, though the counterargument is that presumably facial recognition, fingerprint identification, and allied biometrics could serve as validation. Some though fret that this could serve as an alarming prospect for large-scale privacy intrusion.

Another concern is that cyber-hacking could intercept a vote and change it, for which we might not know that such illegitimate and illegal vote changes have taken place. This becomes a version of an electronic interloper, either done by a human working remotely or perhaps carried out by a devilish automated chatbot or equivalent.

And, believe it or not, you might still have the "helper" misgivings that arise with paper-based ballots, namely that a person comes to the voter and offers to assist them in casting their electronic vote. Sitting with the voter at a laptop or computer screen, or perhaps while voting on a smartphone, you can easily envision that the interloper could do many of the same dubious acts as they might do with paper-based ballots, despite the use of electronic voting.

Generally, it seems that we are likely to be casting votes via vote-by-mail for a while longer and unlikely that we will go online on a widespread basis anytime soon, plus when we do go online there will still be rancorous debates about the legitimacy of the votes and the voting process.

There does not seem to be any free lunch in resolving the matter of voting in elections.

Here's an intriguing question: *Would the advent of AI-based true self-driving cars make a difference in the voting process, and if so, might self-driving cars help or hinder things?*

Let's unpack the matter and see.

The Levels Of Self-Driving Cars

True self-driving cars are ones that the AI drives the car entirely on its own and there isn't any human assistance during the driving task.

These driverless vehicles are considered a Level 4 and Level 5, while a car that requires a human driver to co-share the driving effort is usually considered at a Level 2 or Level 3. The cars that co-share the driving task are described as being semi-autonomous, and typically contain a variety of automated add-on's that are referred to as ADAS (Advanced Driver-Assistance Systems).

There is not yet a true self-driving car at Level 5, which we don't yet even know if this will be possible to achieve, and nor how long it will take to get there.

Meanwhile, the Level 4 efforts are gradually trying to get some traction by undergoing very narrow and selective public roadway trials, though there is controversy over whether this testing should be allowed per se (we are all life-or-death guinea pigs in an experiment taking place on our highways and byways, some point out).

Since semi-autonomous cars require a human driver, the adoption of those types of cars won't be markedly different than driving conventional vehicles, so there's not much new per se to cover about them on this topic (though, as you'll see in a moment, the points next made are generally applicable).

For semi-autonomous cars, it is important that the public needs to be forewarned about a disturbing aspect that's been arising lately, namely that in spite of those human drivers that keep posting videos of themselves falling asleep at the wheel of a Level 2 or Level 3 car, we all need to avoid being misled into believing that the driver can take away their attention from the driving task while driving a semi-autonomous car.

You are the responsible party for the driving actions of the vehicle, regardless of how much automation might be tossed into a Level 2 or Level 3.

Self-Driving Cars And Voting

For Level 4 and Level 5 true self-driving vehicles, there won't be a human driver involved in the driving task.

All occupants will be passengers.

The AI is doing the driving.

That is certainly interesting and somewhat exciting, but you might be perplexed as to why the advent of self-driving cars is somehow related to the topic of vote-by-mail.

They seem to be on entirely different plains or disjoint from each other.

Not so.

Keep in mind that the underlying theme or element of the vote-by-mail topic is the nature of mobility.

Yes, hidden within the vote-by-mail discussion and bitter debate is the matter of mobility, which arose by pointing out that part of the reason for the ballot being mailed to the home is that it aids in undercutting the need to get to a polling place to cast a vote.

Pundits believe that the emergence of AI-based true self-driving cars will be a boon for those that today are mobility disadvantaged. It is hoped that the cost of using cars will radically decrease, presumably partially and to a great extent due to the removal of the need for a human driver, which is an added labor cost and also a logistical barrier too.

It is said that we will finally have mobility-for-all.

In that case, the friction involved in being able to get to a polling place would be dramatically reduced, moving toward being more seamless, though let's be realistic and agree that there will nonetheless still be some difficulties and hurdles to deal with.

The point being that the use of self-driving cars could reinvigorate the use of polling places, at least on the basis of enabling the mobility side of the equation (obviously, this does not negate the potential post-pandemic concerns about people gathering together, etc.)

At the same time, self-driving cars could further enable the vote-by-mail process.

How so?

Imagine that a self-driving car goes into a neighborhood and goes from home to home, stopping to get any ballots cast by those at those homes.

The AI is doing the driving and for the moment let's assume that no one is inside the vehicle.

In that case, there is no interloper that can somehow sway the voting act, and the self-driving car is merely a means of picking up the ballots. The self-driving car then dutifully and eventually drives to an official receiving center and delivers the ballots. In theory, no human hands touch the ballots during that delivery process, other than the voters that have cast the ballots.

When I refer to self-driving cars, please realize that this kind of pick-up and delivery could be something other than a passenger car.

There are lots of self-driving delivery vehicles that are already emerging, oftentimes much smaller than a conventional sized car. Thus, the self-driving vehicle might not even have any provision to carry human passengers and solely be used as a pick-up and delivery agent.

The smarmy response would be that someone might do something untoward by grabbing out a ballot that another neighbor put into the vehicle, but this is readily solved by having a deposit box as part of the vehicle. Once a ballot is placed into the locked box, no one else can retrieve it, until the self-driving car reaches the official delivery center where the key to unlocking it would be kept.

Admittedly one downside is the so-called "last mile" of how to have a self-driving car that is parked at the curb be accessible to someone that is in their home and perhaps is unable to physically come out to the curb itself. But this is already a known shipping problem for goods delivery of any kind and there is a multitude of efforts underway to solve it, including robots that either walk or roll-up to the door.

In short, self-driving cars would make it easier to undertake voting by mail, though many aspects would still need to be ironed out, and meanwhile the onset of self-driving cars would also further enable voting at polling places if that's what society wished to do.

Conclusion

Sorry to say that there are other underbelly aspects too in the matter of self-driving cars and the voting process.

Human interlopers could still be involved.

In fact, the odds are that those "helpers" would be even more readily able to perform their acts since they would have a convenient form of mobility to do so.

With today's interlopers, they either need to know how to drive or need to find someone that will drive them to the homes for their interloping acts (well, some might use bicycles or walk, but by-and-large it is car-based, one presumes).

In the future, any such interloper becomes merely a passenger, not needing a driver's license and nor deal with arranging for a human driver.

It just goes to show that humanity is still humanity, regardless of the addition of AI into the formula.

If you believe that these "helpers" are providing a valuable service, you would undoubtedly welcome and be ecstatic that self-driving cars will become their trusted steed and carry them to-and-fro for their noble acts.

If you doubt the efficacy of these interlopers, you would presumably have a distaste for self-driving cars as an enabler, though this might be balanced by the other benefits of self-driving cars toward being the collector of vote-by-mail ballots and for boosting the chances of people coming to polling places.

As I said before, there isn't any free lunch in any of this, and the societal plusses and minuses are going to continue unabated, including being intricately intertwined with the miraculous advent of self-driving cars.

.

.

CHAPTER 9
APOLLO 12 LESSONS
AND
AI SELF-DRIVING CARS

Dr. Lance B. Eliot

CHAPTER 9

APOLLO 12 LESSONS AND
AI SELF-DRIVING CARS

This is an exciting week for space travel and kudos goes to NASA and SpaceX for being on the verge of launching astronauts into space from U.S. soil after about a decade long hiatus of doing so, along with a first-time foray into using a private company to perform such an exhilarating and breathtaking feat.

Perhaps we might take a moment to reflect upon our prior space travel and amazingly awe-inspiring launches that have inevitably put us on a course that has led to these latest opportunities.

Consider, if you will, the case of Apollo 12.

I refer to Apollo 12 as the middle child, for the following reasons.

By the way, when you are the middle child in a family, the odds are that you often end up being neglected and not getting the acclaim and glory that your siblings seem to accrue.

This same middle-child invisibility syndrome can be applied to the Apollo 12 mission.

How so?

Well, we all know that Apollo 11 was exceedingly famous for having landed us for the first time ever on the moon.

Apollo 13 was extraordinarily famous for dealing with a mission-altering on-board calamity that forced efforts into a do-or-die rescue and overshadowed the fact that the planned moon landing was not able to occur.

What about Apollo 12?

Most people have little recall of Apollo 12.

They vaguely realize that Apollo 12 also landed on the moon, and it was a relief at the time since it showcased that Apollo 11 was not a mere fluke or happenstance. In essence, after Apollo 11, not everyone was convinced that we could consistently land on the moon and it was thought by some that the first-ever moon landing might not ever happen again.

Yet, along comes Apollo 12, dutifully proving that the Apollo 11 success was more than a one-shot and that we could repeatedly perform the "pull a rabbit out of a hat" magic trick that involved getting humans onto another planet.

It seems doubtful though that anything specific comes to mind when asking someone about the nature or travails of Apollo 12.

For Apollo 12, there was in fact a mighty tense moment that arose during the lift-off, causing quite a sense of inner angst among the astronauts and ground control.

Within less than a minute of having initially launched and with the rockets blazing a path skyward, the entire mission was on the verge of being scrubbed, potentially doing so to save the astronauts and avoid what seemed to be a possibly cataclysmic outcome while only at the opening start of the long-haul ahead.

Had that unfortunate scrub taken place, imagine the reaction worldwide.

Though presumably and hopefully the astronauts would have been saved by the use of the jettison procedures, the mission as a whole would have been seen as a failure.

We were in a Cold War-era, including having a fierce "domination" competition going on with the Russians over the control of outer space, and undoubtedly the lack of an Apollo 12 moon landing would have given an added edge to those that contended we were a one-trick pony on being able to get to the moon and conquer space travel.

If the Apollo 13 mission had then subsequently taken place and, as you know, it decidedly did not make a moon landing, there would have been a lot of egg on our face from having both Apollo 12 and Apollo 13 go afoul.

In recap, in this historical revisionist perspective, we would have scrubbed the Apollo 12 mission in the first minute or two of launch, and then have "scrubbed" the Apollo 13 mission after getting nearly midway to the moon (having to come back to earth without landing on the moon).

One doubts that there would have been much zeal or support remaining from the public and by regulators with the purse strings to continue these seemingly fruitless moon-going missions.

The billions of dollars pouring in the space program would have come under heightened scrutiny. Besides the exorbitant costs, some at the time questioned why we were seeking to go to the moon, and also questioned the jeopardy being placed upon the lives of the astronauts.

All in all, if Apollo 12 had been stopped at that fateful minute or two into the flight, one can say that we might have had the later toils of Apollo 13 and then the entire space program would have been halted.

No more efforts to get to the moon.

And, likely a complete disruption and slowdown in any progress on our space venturing efforts.

In that overarching context, I trust that you can see that those opening minutes of the Apollo 12 launch had a lot more historical importance than otherwise the press or media has seemingly covered.

I'll get to the harrowing details in a moment.

Speaking of tense moments, let's not forget that even the siblings of Apollo 12 had them too, and you might remember the traumatic tensions that occurred in Apollo 11 and in Apollo 13 (well, Apollo 13 was nearly all about tensions, especially once the mid-flight difficulties ensued).

You might recall that Apollo 11 had some pretty tense moments when the lunar lander was on its approach to the surface of the moon (see my explanation of the incident and lessons learned for self-driving cars, at this **link here**).

In the case of Apollo 11, a systems error occurred, infamously known as the Error Code 1202, and was assessed in a heart-pounding scrape by ground control, declaring it to be an issue that could be ignored, permitting the moon landing to occur without needing to abandon the quest.

Apollo 13 obviously had even more egregious and heart palpitating troubles (see my description and a detailed look at what really happened, along with providing lessons learned for self-driving cars, at **this link here**).

Okay, so Apollo 11 and Apollo 13 both had tense moments, famously so, and thus perhaps it is time to make clear-cut that Apollo 12 also had a notable tense moment, occurring just as the mission got barely underway.

If you are looking for lessons learned from all of these gotchas or glitches, one immediate point to be made apparent is that for any complex system the odds are high that something will go awry.

As such, it is best to anticipate that things will indeed go awry and try to be as prepared to deal with those occurrences as you can be so readied for.

Plus, of course, seek to construct any complex system in such a manner that any awry conditions are detected as quickly as possible, along with having some kind of built-in recovery or resiliency in anticipation of Murphy's Law driven incidences.

I have specific lessons gleaned about the Apollo 12 awry incident and will be getting to those after first establishing the context as to what happened overall.

Apollo 12 And The SCE To Aux

During the morning of November 14, 1969, the rain was coming down upon the launch area of Apollo 12.

Despite the rainfall, weather forecasts suggested that the rain would not impede the liftoff and so the mission continue ahead unabated.

The flight team consisted of Astronaut Charles "Pete" Conrad commanding the flight and had Astronaut Richard Gordon (designated to be the Command Module pilot) and Astronaut Alan Bean (designated to be the Lunar Module pilot), working together for the mission.

After the usual countdown, the rocket engines roared to life and the spacecraft inched its way off the launchpad.

So far, so good, but get ready for the twist of fate that was about to occur.

At about 36 seconds after liftoff, the spacecraft was struck by lightning, and another bolt struck again at about 52 seconds.

When the lightning strikes zapped the rocket ship, the astronauts at that time were not fully aware that it had happened, and nor was the ground control aware per se (note that afterward, during post-mission analyses, recorded video, and other aspects demonstrably showcase the lightning strikes).

Here's a snippet of the official time-stamped transcript based on their voice utterings at the 37 seconds mark of the flight:
00:37 Gordon (onboard):   "What the hell was that?"
00:38 Conrad (onboard):   "Huh?"
00:39 Gordon (onboard):   "I lost a whole bunch of stuff; I don't know..."

Then, at the one-minute mark, following the second lightning strike:

01:02 Conrad: "Okay, we just lost the platform, gang. I don't know what happened here; we had everything in the world drop out."

The displays in the spacecraft cockpit were illuminating like a Christmas tree, providing a slew of alarms and blinking frantically to alert the crew:

01:12 Conrad: "I got three fuel cell lights, an AC bus light, a fuel cell disconnect, AC bus overload 1 and 2, Main Bus A and B out."

Notably, it was post-mission stated that during the hundreds of simulations conducted beforehand of various spacecraft issues that might arise, none of the scenarios tested with the astronauts involved an entire plethora of alarms and nor button blinking of the likes that occurred during this actual flight.

We'll come back to that point shortly.

You can imagine how unsettling the matter must have been in real-time, namely being presented in live flight with something that had not ever been simulated and for which came completely by surprise and without any semblance of what it might portend.

And, disturbingly taking place just moments after launch, within about a minute of finally having gotten underway.

Upon some back-and-forth among the astronauts and interaction with ground control, none of which was seemingly able to resolve the now mystifying condition, and which was still taking place for a distressingly long 20 seconds or so, here's what ground control's Gerald Carr relayed to the astronauts:

01:36 Carr: "Apollo 12, Houston. Try SCE to Auxiliary. Over."

For clarification, the SCE was the Signal Conditioning Equipment, a piece of equipment inside the spacecraft that essentially brought together electronic messages coming from other parts of the craft and conditioned or filtered them for purposes of then sharing into other onboard systems such as the telemetry indicator (an 8-ball that roved around in its sphere to highlight position related status).

On the cockpit display board in front of the astronauts, there was an entire gaggle of switches, including some relatively obscures ones associated with the SCE. The SCE was not especially a component that had been emphasized during flight training, and generally was one of those internal pieces of electronics that few figured would likely require the attention of the astronauts.

One setting for SCE was to have it make use of an auxiliary power source, and a switch existed to allow the astronauts to make that switchover, though normally there would not be any special reason to do so.

In fact, it was assumed to be an extremely rare chance that the switch and the use of auxiliary would ever be needed and unlikely too to be of value in a breathtaking urgency, it was just not something that was particularly in the minds of the astronauts, as the dialogue next illustrates:

01:39 Conrad: "Try FCE to Auxiliary."
01:41 Conrad (onboard):   "What the hell is that?"
01:42 Gordon (onboard):   "Fuel cell..."

You can see that the SCE was so out-of-mind that they thought the instruction was about the fuel cells, which would have been a topic more likely to be at the forefront of their thinking.

Ground control quickly intervened to repeat the instruction:

01:43 Carr: "SCE, SCE to auxiliary."
01:45 Conrad (onboard):   "Try the buses. Get the buses back on the line."

Amazingly, happily, the mere switching of SCE to the Auxiliary power source did the trick:

01:48 Bean (onboard):   "It looks - Everything looks good."
01:50 Conrad (onboard):   "SCE to Aux."

The matter was resolved.

At the time, the astronauts had no notion of why the switchover resolved the matter, and nor did most of the ground control know either.

There was just one person that had proffered the suggestion to make the switch of SCE to Aux, and his name is John Aaron, ultimately nicknamed the *steely-eyed missile man*.

Born in 1943, he was a youngster of just 26 years old when sitting in the flight controller seat as the Chief EECOM Officer at ground control for Apollo 12, meaning that he was responsible for knowing about and troubleshooting (from the ground) the Electrical, Environmental and Communications (EECOM) systems of the spacecraft.

He certainly did his job that morning on November 14, 1969.

But, how did he know that the astronauts needed to do the "SCE to Aux" action?

As a quick aside, the phrase of "SCE to Aux" or sometimes indicated as SCE-to-Aux has since then become well-known amongst engineers and tech wizards as a shorthand for meaning that sometimes you need to know the one trick or one key step to take when solving a problem, especially those maddeningly harried problems that have you on edge (reminiscent of the fable or joke about knowing where to tap, based ostensibly on a story about Henry Ford and Charles Steinmetz).

John Aaron later indicated that he guessed at the use of SCE-to-Aux because of the plethora of alarms and blinking lights that the astronauts reported seeing, along with his own inspection of his computer screen at ground control.

He had seen that pattern before.

As the story goes, during a simulation with one of the back-up crews on a third-shift late-night and altogether routine kind of practice, many months earlier, there had been an inadvertent overload of power, producing the same set of alarms, blinking lights, and a resultant data display at his screen. Others at the time were apparently embarrassed at the mistaken effort that led to the power issues.

Because it was a readily apparent power-related issue, it seemed prudent to switch the SCE to Aux, and the problem seemed resolved about the alarms and blinking lights.

Meanwhile, he was particularly intrigued at seeing those "squirrely numbers" on his display (rather than merely expecting all zeros) and tried the next day to dig more deeply into the matter. In any case, though he did not know for sure what would lead to such a problem, he otherwise let the matter be filed away in his mind, though not realizing or necessarily anticipating whether it would ever be needed again.

It did!

Sure enough, during those crucial 20 seconds on the morning of November 14, 1969, he studied his display and thought about how it all seemed to fit the pattern he had once seen, and so decided that it was worth a chance to make the SCE-to-Aux switchover. The downside risk seemed to be relatively low, while the upside potential seemed to be high.

Once the SCE-to-Aux switchover resolved things, the astronauts a few minutes later were able to be reflective about what had just happened, and jokingly suggested that the crisis moment had been a type of simulation (which, obviously it was not).

Here's what was said about the matter at about 4 minutes into the flight:

04:07 Conrad: " Hey, that's one of the better SIM's, believe me."
04:12 Conrad (onboard): "Phew! Man alive! I'll tell you what happened..."

It was a brief but memorable moment, dwarfed one would say by the mission ultimately landing on the moon and returning safely to earth.

Sometimes the devil though is in the details.

Let's unpack the matter and see what lessons can be learned.

Lessons Learned From The SCE-To-Aux Of Apollo 12

I'll extract several key lessons from the Apollo 12 incident involving SCE-to-Aux.

In addition, it will be handy to apply those lessons to a modern-day aspect, showcasing that the lessons from fifty years ago are still applicable to today's state-of-the-art systems.

We can use AI-based true self-driving cars as an exemplar for considering the lessons learned.

True self-driving cars are ones that the AI drives the car entirely on its own and there isn't any human assistance during the driving task.

These driverless vehicles are considered a Level 4 and Level 5, while a car that requires a human driver to co-share the driving effort is usually considered at a Level 2 or Level 3. The cars that co-share the driving task are described as being semi-autonomous, and typically contain a variety of automated add-on's that are referred to as ADAS (Advanced Driver-Assistance Systems).

Here are my gleaned and re-applied lessons:

- **Importance of simulations**

Were it not for the use of simulations, John Aaron would seemingly not have known about the SCE-to-Aux "solution" per se for dealing with the alarms and blinking lights.

This highlights the importance of utilizing simulations, especially for complex systems.

For the advent of AI-based self-driving cars, simulations are a must.

All of the contenders seeking self-driving car capabilities are running simulations daily and expending a tremendous amount of cost and effort toward doing so.

Rightfully so.

Some argue that they should be doing even more.

- **Leveraging simulations that go awry**

Per John Aaron's account, the simulation that led him to the SCE-to-Aux aspect was not intending to do so, and instead, the simulation had somewhat gone awry.

Of course, the preferred place to have things go awry is during a simulation, rather than when the actual system is underway.

Thus, for those doing simulations for AI self-driving cars, do not downplay or disregard when your simulations have hiccups or produce quirky results.

It might be fate handing you a favor.

- **Forcing simulations to go awry**

The discussion of simulations brings up another point that might seem odd.

When you are doing simulations, you ought to intentionally seek to make things go rather untoward.

I say this because oftentimes those doing simulations stick with the tried-and-true and do not consider wild or outside-the-box scenarios.

Those ostensibly crazy and improbable possibilities need to be on the To-Do list and not simply perchance arise by a "by mistake" occurrence.

- **Need for being inquisitive**

John Aaron's inquisitive nature led him to explore the discrepancy that happened during the simulation. Most people probably would have shrugged it off and not thought one wit more about it.

For the hiring of AI developers, aim during hiring to seek out ones that have an innate inquisitiveness, and then foster that sense of curiosity while on-the-job and crafting AI systems such as self-driving cars.

The payoff will be substantive.

- **Availability and timeliness of knowledge**

Suppose that John Aaron wasn't sitting in the EECOM seat at ground control and might have been assigned other duties, elsewhere and not in the midst of the flight activities.

What then?

It seems that whoever was in the seat might not have perchance known the SCE-to-Aux aspect.

How long would the flight have continued forward with the alarms and blinking lights, and might the unknown nature of the problem have caused everyone to conclude that it was prudent to scrub the mission right then and there, for which as I've stated earlier would have potentially altered history in dramatic ways?

AI developers for complex systems such as self-driving cars have a lot of knowledge locked away in their minds about the nuances of the autonomous capabilities, including what's happening in the Machine Learning (ML) and Deep Learning (DL) components.

Firms crafting self-driving cars need to consider how to make that knowledge explicitly documented, along with being available at the touch-of-a-finger, which might be crucial if some self-driving cars suddenly go awry.

- **Role of trust in especially time-exigent situations**

During the flight predicament, when John Aaron indicated to relay the instruction about switching the SCE-to-Aux, it was apparently a surprise to the other ground control personnel and they were unsure of why he was making such a suggestion.

The astronauts too were obviously somewhat taken aback.

Nobody though opted to argue about the matter, which would have taken precious time to do, and assumed or presumed that the instruction was worthy of carrying out.

This comes not by happenstance but by building up trust.

For those firms making and fielding AI-based self-driving cars, be mindful of the importance of building trust among your teams, crossing the often presumptive domain-gulf that occurs between the AI developers and the operations side of the business.

Conclusion

Apollo 12 was a miracle that deserves its place alongside the miracles of Apollo 11 and Apollo 13.

Do not deny the middle child its due.

If you are asked to side with one child over the other, any caring parent would tell you that all of their children are precious and valued, equally so.

The same can be said about each of the Apollo space missions.

.

CHAPTER 10

RUNNING OVER SHOOTER
AND
AI SELF-DRIVING CARS

CHAPTER 10

RUNNING OVER SHOOTER

AND

AI SELF-DRIVING CARS

Quite a harrowing moment occurred recently when a man with a rifle started randomly shooting at people while standing on the Centennial Bridge in Leavenworth, Missouri.

A Kansas soldier that happened to be driving his car on the bridge, while then waiting in traffic, realized that an active shooter was ahead of him, and so the soldier opted to navigate his car out of traffic and steered directly toward the shooter, ramming smackdab into him.

The shooter was knocked over and no longer able to shoot.

When police arrived, they and responding medical personnel extracted the shooter from underneath the soldier's car and took the injured shooter to a nearby Kansas City hospital.

There is no doubt that the solider saved lives.

He is a hero.

His quick response and alert mindfulness stopped the shooter and prevented further potential carnage.

It was a prudent act and one that required quick thinking.

One supposes that some people in a similar circumstance would have tried to duck down inside their car to avoid getting shot. Or, maybe tried to put their car immediately into reverse, and backed-up to try and get away from the scene. Perhaps even gotten out of their car and run desperately for safety. For an explanation of ways to deal with outdoor active shooters while you are inside a vehicle such as a car or a bus.

In this case, the soldier reasoned that he could take swift action to end the shooting spree, doing so by using whatever resource might be readily available in the situation, which was his car.

Not everyone would have had such a first thought, namely that their car could be used as a type of defensive weapon to defuse the situation.

Most of us instinctively do everything possible to avoid hitting anyone with our vehicle.

If a jaywalking pedestrian suddenly darts into the street, you will instantly hit the brakes and come to a screeching halt, a type of reflexive action based on years of driving. Similarly, when a bicyclist veers in front of your car at an intersection, you likely would radically swerve to avoid hitting the interloper.

In short, we have been trained and have experience in seeking to avert ramming into people, which is reinforced nearly every day that you take your car for a drive.

Again and again, you have ongoing moments while driving on even a daily journey of intentionally avoiding people that might perchance be in the vicinity of your car, whether they are in the middle of the street, or stepping off the sidewalk, or jogging through an unmarked crosswalk.

Of course, there are those crazy drivers that get into a road rage mindset and decide to smash other cars or attempt to run over people.

There are also those rather rare circumstances when the brakes on a car suddenly fail and the driver is unable to control their vehicle, sadly sometimes bashing into an innocent bystander.

And, there are way too many instances of drunk drivers that smash into pedestrians or otherwise are driving out-of-control and injure or kill people that happen to be in the wrong place at the wrong time.

The point overall though is that on a societal and cultural basis, we are instinctively geared toward not hitting people, along with being aware of criminal laws that make doing so a harshly punishable act, and thus on a normal daily basis, we pretty much do not run over people (statistically, that would be true, given that we drive in the U.S. some 3.2 trillion miles annually and have relatively few pedestrian deaths or injuries for all of that voluminous driving, though each such injury or death is certainly tragic and ought to be avoided).

Would you have made a real-time instantaneous decision to ram the shooter?

I dare say that most of us would like to think that we would have done so, but trying to overcome the years of habit about not striking people is not so easily conquered, and especially without any warning or heads-up that such an act is unexpectedly warranted and imminently needed.

The solider indicated to a reporter that he had prior training on active shooter situations overall, which likely did help in his quick reaction decision-making, and yet you never know whether prior training will kick-in and motivate sufficiently at the requisite moment.

There is a bit of twist on this overall topic about the use of our cars.

We are supposed to not use our vehicles to harm others, a seemingly sacrosanct principle.

But I think we all would agree that the soldier did the right thing by using his car to harm the active shooter.

In short, the hard-and-fast rule about never using your car to strike others is actually more bendable than might otherwise seem to be the case.

It is societally agreeable and legally acceptable to use your car as a means to harm someone in certain kinds of situations, as this example of the active shooter getting put down well-instructively showcases.

Ponder that for a moment.

We are in the midst of AI-based self-driving cars being readied for use on our public roadways, and one facet that is not yet resolved involves how the AI is supposed to act in all of the myriads of driving situations that might arise.

This brings up an intriguing question: *Would an AI-based true self-driving car have been "savvy" enough to run over an active shooter, but at the same time not runover people-at-large whenever it seemed like the potentially right thing to do and yet might not really be?*

In other words, do we want AI systems to "decide" to run people over, injuring or potentially killing those human beings?

That's a tough nut to crack.

Let's unpack the matter and see.

The Role of AI-Based Self-Driving Cars

True self-driving cars are ones that the AI drives the car entirely on its own and there isn't any human assistance during the driving task.

These driverless vehicles are considered a Level 4 and Level 5, while a car that requires a human driver to co-share the driving effort is usually considered at a Level 2 or Level 3. The cars that co-share the driving task are described as being semi-autonomous, and typically contain a variety of automated add-on's that are referred to as ADAS (Advanced Driver-Assistance Systems).

There is not yet a true self-driving car at Level 5, which we don't yet even know if this will be possible to achieve, and nor how long it will take to get there.

Meanwhile, the Level 4 efforts are gradually trying to get some traction by undergoing very narrow and selective public roadway trials, though there is controversy over whether this testing should be allowed per se (we are all life-or-death guinea pigs in an experiment taking place on our highways and byways, some point out).

Since semi-autonomous cars require a human driver, the adoption of those types of cars won't be markedly different than driving conventional vehicles, so there's not much new per se to cover about them on this topic (though, as you'll see in a moment, the points next made are generally applicable).

For semi-autonomous cars, it is important that the public needs to be forewarned about a disturbing aspect that's been arising lately, namely that in spite of those human drivers that keep posting videos of themselves falling asleep at the wheel of a Level 2 or Level 3 car, we all need to avoid being misled into believing that the driver can take away their attention from the driving task while driving a semi-autonomous car.

You are the responsible party for the driving actions of the vehicle, regardless of how much automation might be tossed into a Level 2 or Level 3.

Self-Driving Cars And The Law

For Level 4 and Level 5 true self-driving vehicles, there won't be a human driver involved in the driving task.

All occupants will be passengers.

The AI is doing the driving.

One of the biggest worries that the public has about AI-based self-driving cars is that those vehicles need to be driven in a safe manner.

Generally, the hope is that the AI driving systems will be as safe as or even safer than human drivers.

Currently, in the United States alone, there are some 40,000 deaths annually due to car crashes, and about 2.3 million injuries that occur as a result of car accidents. Human drivers have known foibles such as driving when distracted, driving when intoxicated, etc. The assumption is that the AI will not be drinking, it won't be distracted, and so overall it ought to be a safer driver than human drivers.

We do not yet know whether this will be the case.

One thing that we do know is that a key precept for AI driving systems is that they are not supposed to ram into people.

Via the use of various sensory devices, including cameras, radar, LIDAR, ultrasonic devices, and the like, an AI system is supposed to be scrutinizing all the data about what is surrounding the vehicle. In that morass of info, the AI has to tease out the aspect that there are pedestrians nearby, or that a bicyclist is getting close to the car, and so on. And, upon making such detections, not hit those people.

Presumably, the AI has been intentionally crafted to avoid striking any of those nearby humans.

That seems prudent.

This sensible principle might remind you of the famous *Three Laws of Robotics* that were devised by science fiction writer Issac Asimov in 1942, of which those "laws" have become lore subsequently, including that the first rule says this: "A robot may not injure a human being or, through inaction, allow a human being to come to harm."

We have all grown accustomed to the Asimov rules and have seen them energetically portrayed in numerous big-time movies and TV shows.

A reality check is needed about those so-called laws.

They are not laws in any conventional meaning of the word "laws" and therefore please do not be somehow misled.

For example, some people at times think that an AI driving system will never ever hit a person via the self-driving car because it would break the Asimov "law" about not injuring a human being. In essence, this is a false belief that the Asimov rule is akin to a law of physics or a law of chemistry, as though there are nature-imposed limitations that cannot be exceeded or broken, because, well, because that is the way nature is.

There is absolutely nothing at all that prevents an AI system from ramming into a person, other than the coding or programming of the AI to try and prevent such an act.

Also, let's cover the topic of sentience while we are on this matter.

The goal of AI is to ultimately achieve the equivalent of human intelligence, which, notably, we are not anywhere yet near to accomplishing. In addition, some assert that the vaunted version of AI will become sentient, thus instilling the same ill-defined spark that humanity and living creatures appear to embody. In theory, it is thought that this sentience might arrive at the moment of the singularity, a point in time at which AI seemingly gains revered sentience.

We do not know if sentience is possible for computationally machine-based AI.

No one knows too whether this notion of a singularity is going to occur, nor when it might occur.

In any case, for those that believe in sentience and the singularity, they at times might also suggest that once this happens, the AI will "know" that killing people is a wrong thing to do. Prior to that point in time, presumably, the AI was (hopefully) programmed to not do such acts, but it did not "understand" the provision and was merely abiding programmatically.

I don't want to go too far on this tangent, but we ought to at least agree that even if the AI reaches sentience, there is no particular reason it will opt to not run into people. Humans run into people. If AI is going to be akin to human intelligence, doesn't it seem plausible that AI might run into people?

There is both the smiley face version of the singularity outcome, in which AI is a great benefactor to humanity and the sad face version of AI as humanity-crushing and enslaving evildoer, along with numerous variants in-between those polar extremes (for more on such speculation, see my **analysis here**).

Moving on, another variant involved in this discussion is the role of intent.

If an AI driving system runs into someone, did it intend to do so?

That is a murky topic.

Some would say that if the AI was programmed to allow for ramming into people, ergo it evidently was built with the "intention" to be able to do so and therefore unequivocally exhibits intent.

Others would decry this kind of argument and proffer that intent is only possible with sentient beings. Thus, until or if AI crosses over into sentience, it never has any semblance of "intent" per se.

The matter of intention is a whole another can of worms to be dealt with regarding AI.

AI And The Runover Someone Dilemma

Return to the story of the solider that ran over the active shooter.

In that situation, we applaud the human driver for doing so.

Imagine that you were sitting in a self-driving car, while on that bridge, while the active shooter was shooting his rifle.

Would you want the AI to proceed to ram into the active shooter?

It seems like we would want that kind of action, since, as we now know, it stopped the active shooter from his dastardly act.

But, this would quite obviously violate the science fiction rule of a robot not causing injury to a human being.

Oops, a contradiction.

You might counterargue that the same rule also offers that through inaction the robot is not allowed to have a human come to harm.

Thus, if the AI driving system opted to <u>not</u> run over the shooter, and assuming the shooter kept shooting and harming people, the inaction of the AI would lead to humans being harmed.

Therefore, the AI indeed should run over the shooter.

That seems to clear-up the matter.

Does it?

You are opening a Pandora's box, some would say.

If you believe that the AI driving system should run over the shooter, you are indicating that it is okay for the AI to use the self-driving car to harm humans.

Now that you've opened that door, the question arises about how far to keep it open and what will be the means of trying to shut that door.

We all agree in retrospect that the active shooter was doing a wrongful act and needed to be stopped. That though is quite a sizable amount of logic and interpretation.

Consider the myriad of circumstances that might arise about when we would agree that the use of a car to harm someone was warranted or not warranted.

An AI system that has been programmed or coded, and presumably not yet sentient, would have to embody a slew of facets about human ethics, human laws, societal norms, and the rest.

Keep in mind that currently there is no such thing as common-sense reasoning for AI, other than prototypes and small examples (see my **discussion here**), and thus you cannot just load-in an AI-based common sense component to help make these kinds of decisions (some lump this into the re-phrased and reborn notion of AI, known as Artificial General Intelligence or AGI).

Note too that such a decision was made in real-time.

The solider did not call others to confer about what to do. He made a choice on-the-spot. The point being that if you suggest that we can allow AI to proceed on such matters, but first it would need to seek advice or permission, the question arises about how that would work in any real-time situation.

Some might point out that if there was a passenger in the self-driving car, during the unfolding of the shooting event, the AI could simply ask the human passenger what the AI ought to do.

Indeed, this brings up Asimov's second rule: "A robot must obey the orders given it by human beings except where such orders would conflict with the First Law."

Okay, so assume that the human passenger tells the AI to ram the shooter, or maybe the AI offers that it would be willing to ram the shooter and wants approval from the human passenger.

The human passenger yells out, yes, runover that no-good son-of-a-gun and the AI heroically proceeds.

Well, we already have a conflict with respect to the Asimov rules, since the command by the human is telling the AI to harm another human, which seems like a violation.

Though there is the angle that the running over of the shooter will likely save other humans, how is such an aspect to be known, and it seems like quite a judgment to make (in this case, a right one, but not necessarily always so)?

It seems that asking the human passenger might have resolved the dilemma.

Unfortunately, no, it does not.

First, suppose the human passenger was a child that was riding alone in the self-driving car (this will indeed be happening, likely quite often), and do you want a child making such a decision or even being placed into a posture of having to make such decisions?

Second, suppose there weren't any passengers in the self-driving car, which will likely be the case much of the time as self-driving cars are roaming around looking to be available for those that need a lift. In that circumstance, there is not a human available in the car to provide any direction on the matter.

Third, you might argue that a remote assistant could be accessed, such as an OnStar-like human agent, but do you want a person that is not at the scene to make such a decision, and for which the remote access might not happen at all or be delayed due to connectivity issues.

Here's the part that will likely send chills down your back.

If we did decide that a human passenger could make such decisions, how far might that be stretched, and veer perilously into a decidedly undesirable realm?

Imagine that a human passenger sees someone that they've always disliked, and the person is merely walking across the street, no weapons, purely innocently out for a stroll, and the rider in the self-driving car falsely urges the AI driving system to run over that person, claiming that the pedestrian is a threat.

Now what?

Do we really expect the AI to discern which situations are valid for a runover and which are not?

Conclusion

Bringing things back to today's reality, most AI self-driving cars being formulated currently would not on-their-own seek to run over that active shooter, and in fact, the AI system is likely to have various programmatic precautions to vigorously attempt to avoid hitting a person (any and all persons).

Nor would the Natural Language Processing (NLP) in-car interactive component somehow allow for a human rider to instruct the AI to proceed to ram the shooter.

In short, the self-driving car and the AI would have done nothing in that situation, other than wait for the traffic to proceed.

Admittedly, this whole discussion can be labeled as an edge case or corner case, meaning it will only happen rarely and for the automakers and self-driving tech makers it just isn't something on their busy plate right now (i.e., the aim at this time is fundamentally getting a self-driving car that can safely navigate everyday street driving scenarios).

At some point, as a society, we are going to need to have a really serious talk about what we expect AI and especially self-driving cars to do, including the act of running over humans, which seems like an ironclad no-no, but the real-world is a lot grayer and confounding than it might seem.

Meanwhile, for that heroic soldier, thanks immensely for your service and mindfulness.

.

.

CHAPTER 11
GRIMES SOUL SEARCHING
AND
AI SELF-DRIVING CARS

CHAPTER 11

GRIMES SOUL SEARCHING
AND
AI SELF-DRIVING CARS

Claire Boucher, popularly known by her artist name of Grimes, opted to put together an art show entitled *Selling Out* that offers her artistry including various prints, drawings, conceptual pieces, and photographs, which might otherwise not have been especially startling or controversial except for one other item that she also decided to put up for sell.

Her soul.

That's right, as part of the effort to showcase her handcrafted talent, she also has opted to sell part of her soul.

Ridiculous, you might exclaim.

A stunt, some might holler.

Not so fast.

In one sense, there is some ironclad logic involved, since she has emphasized that artists routinely put their heart and soul into their work, thus, when selling such artistry, it ergo inextricably has a part of the inner toil or soul of the artist that goes implicitly along with it, wherever the art goes and for the benefit of whoever purchases the earnestly sweat-and-tears cast product.

And if this is indeed the normal case, why not make things clearer and more transparent by directly and explicitly selling part of the artist's soul, which certainly would seem an indubitably above-board way of doing things.

Perhaps this is merely a straightforward matter of rectifying that which is customarily undertaken in a hidden or opaque way into becoming more readily visible and evident.

Case closed.

Plus, lest you have doubts that some portion of her soul is actually going to be conveyed (i.e., no backing out of the deal), Grimes is offering a "legal document" crafted apparently with her attorney that specifies the details, ostensibly laying out the kinds of contractual parameters that you might see when say buying a car or purchasing a home.

This does though make one ponder somewhat.

Imagine the difficulties that might later ensue if the contract is somehow challenged in court, and the type of legal arguments that might be made in either arguing that the matter is completely legal and sound, along with whether the terms of the agreement were fully abided by, such as the portion of soul conveyed as stipulated.

For example, suppose that the contract states that ten percent or maybe twenty percent or some such proportion more-or-less of her soul is being pledged (the percentage has not apparently been announced as yet).

Could the buyer later claim that they did not get the full percentage promised and, if so, how exactly would this be ascertained during a trial?

Maybe things might go in the other direction.

Suppose the buyer somehow took a higher percentage of Grimes's soul than offered in the legal specification, and Grimes wanted to get back that overtaken portion. She might then rightfully sue as a recourse for the overstepped taking, and possibly seek additional damages due to the emotional or spiritual undercutting that the excessive grab produced.

In any case, the soul-selling does provide some of the media with a chance to proffer that this is an over-the-top attempt to bolster the art show, and perhaps that has indeed happened, while others are willing to perceive this as a moment to reflect seriously on the nature of our souls and what it means to refer to the soul itself.

With that last point in mind, let's pursue that angle and see where it takes us.

In addition, one of the beauties of a discussion about the human soul is that it can readily be a segue into another topic that many continue to heatedly debate and fret about, namely the nature of Artificial Intelligence (AI) and whether or not the matter of "soul" is inextricably included.

Elon Musk has been a vocal critic that AI is alarmingly going to eclipse human intelligence and upon doing so might put humanity on the brink of being destroyed.

Musk and Grimes have "Little X" now (the baby's latest naming, per media reporting), and anyone born today will potentially experience advances in AI over the course of their life that might see AI teetering on such dire prophecies, though, for clarity, no one can say when AI might reach sentience, nor whether it ever will, and nor can anyone nail down a date for the asserted singularity that might occur.

There is also an argument to be made that AI might end-up benefiting mankind, possibly saving ourselves from our own self-destruction, and as such, it could be that AI might not be the evildoer that some envision (admittedly, it would certainly seem prudent to keep an eye on the downside condition, given the adverse consequences of getting our clock cleaned, and meanwhile hope for or try to steer things toward the upside option).

As an interesting side tangent, reportedly Musk and Grimes met because of their mutual interest in Roko's Basilisk, a well-known aspect in AI (see my explanation at this link here), and for which she included a character in her *Flesh Without Blood* video that was named Rococo Basilisk, prior to first meeting Musk, so in a sense, you could say that the two of them are AI-kindred spirits.

All told, there is a fascinating convergence on these seemingly disparate topics, encompassing the act of Grime's selling part of her soul, along with where AI is headed in general, combined with Elon Musk's megaphone amplified commentaries about the future of AI, and we can add into this discussion a dollop about the future of self-driving cars for some added measure.

All told, there is a fascinating convergence on these topics, encompassing the act of Grime's selling part of her soul, along with where AI is headed in general, combined with Elon Musk's megaphone amplified commentaries about the future of AI, and we can add into this discussion a dollop about the future of self-driving cars for some added measure.

For those of you that see this as a convoluted and unlikely game of connect-the-dots, it might really be a variant of three-dimensional chess, and there is a rather apparent straight line connecting these matters.

A mashup made in heaven; one might say.

The Soul And What It Is

You would be hard-pressed to irrefutably define what is meant when referring to a soul.

Mankind has generally aligned on the premise that the soul is something embodied in humans and makes them imbued with a certain life-spark as it were or possessing a "je ne sais quoi" indeterminate quality.

From the ancient Greeks, you can trace the word as being tied to the act of breathing, being alive, being functional within the world as a living creature.

In religious terms, the soul is quite vital and an important tenet in nearly everything else that religion might otherwise proffer about beings and life itself.

Philosophers have endlessly discussed and debated the nature of the soul and what it means to have one, and what it means to lack one.

Some believe that only humans can have a soul, while others contend that animals have souls too. Some stop at certain kinds of animals or ones that have particular characteristics, while others assert that insects have souls. You can go even further and claim that bacteria have souls.

There might not be any end in sight per se.

For example, some would suggest that rivers have souls, mountains have souls, etc. Perhaps rocks have souls, maybe even pebbles, and it could be that an itsy-bitsy grain of sand on a wide beach is also infused with a soul. Do atoms have souls? What about sub-atomic particles?

A soul is sometimes said to be immortal, lasting forever. Others believe that a soul exists only as long as the thing itself exists, and once the thing dies or is broken apart, the soul is no longer there.

Many have sought to discover the soul by using scientific techniques and theories.

Perhaps you've heard about the infamous 21 grams aspects about the assumed weight of a soul.

As a quick explanation, a physician in 1907 published the results of an "experiment" that he undertook in trying to figure out the weight of a soul. He assumed that it might be possible to identify and detect how much a soul can weigh.

To ferret this out, he figured that the soul would leave the body upon death, and therefore it seemed obviously forthright to merely weigh someone just at the moment of death, and then compare theirs before and after weight.

This is an example of apparently sincerely seeking to apply scientific principles but messing up badly in the effort to do so.

The entire notion has troubles.

There are some that would argue that the soul does not leave the body at death, and remains intact (thus, there would be no weight loss) and that if he found that there was no weight loss, it cannot confirm and nor disconfirm such a theory and offers nothing of substance about the soul.

Aha, you say, but what if the body does weigh less?

When a body dies, there are numerous changes in the state of the body, for example, a change in body temperature, which can produce an autonomic response of sweating, and this in turn can lead to a weight loss.

In short, there are multiple intervening variables, and trying to perform a simplistic "experiment" is tantamount to ignoring or disrespecting a sound and proper use of the scientific method.

Plus, some would argue that the soul is completely intangible and does not have any semblance of weight associated with it. Some too might argue that the soul is in an entirely different dimension, thus, these experiments in our dimensional world are useless and misguided, unless you could miraculously reach over into that other dimension.

And so on.

Anyway, his approach involved putting dying people onto an industrial-sized weighing scale, each one at a time, atop their respective bed, doing so for six people.

Of the six people, only one seemed to have a loss of weight at death, being "measured" as three-fourths of an ounce, which is about 21.3 grams, which has been commonly rounded to 21 grams.

So, people have doggedly ever since clung to the 21 grams, despite the inadequacies of how it came to be proclaimed.

As an aside, if Grimes has given up perhaps ten percent of her soul, it would mean that she has to give over 2.1 grams worth, while at 20% it would be over 4 grams that would be handed over to the buyer (assuming you concur with the non-scientific and non-sensical twenty-one grams core weight).

Would one dare to give away fifty percent or more (that's a whopping 10 or more grams)?

There are additional weighty questions to contemplate.
- How much of your soul can be given away?
- What are the means by which the soul is extracted and transferred?
- Is there a minimum threshold at which you are no longer soulful and are bereft of your soul?
- Could your soul regrow and replenish the portion that was sold or given away?
- Does the person that receives the soul go over 100% by the mere addition, maybe possessing 23 grams worth of a soul?
- Etc.

AI And The Question Of Soul

Shifting gears, consider the matter of the soul as it relates to AI.

Let's start by agreeing that the overarching goal or aspiration of AI is to develop a computer-based machine that showcases the equivalent of human intelligence (we can somewhat quibble about this definition, such as whether the machine has to be a computer or might be something else, but skip that line of debate for the moment).

Note that such a machine does not necessarily have to be the exact same architecture and structure as a human and nor of the human brain. In other words, we will allow the aims of AI to be able to reach the vaunted AI in whatever manner is feasible, regardless of whether the result is a seeming replica of a human.

Indeed, the AI field often uses a popularized test known as the Turing Test, named after its author the famous Alan Turing, serving as a basis for someday being able to assess whether a true AI has been reached.

The Turing Test is actually quite simple to describe.

Imagine that we put the machine-based AI behind a curtain, and did the same for a human being, and then had a moderator that asked questions of the two. The moderator is not able to see the two contestants and can only judge their answers by their responses. If the moderator ultimately is unable to distinguish between the two, and thus is unable to point out which is the AI and which is the human, it is said that the AI has achieved human intelligence because it is indistinguishable from human intelligence.

The nice aspect of this approach is that you are judging based on the intelligence as exhibited via the answers and dialogue taking place, rather than inspecting how the intelligence has arisen. In short, if I could make an AI that achieved this capability and did so with Lego's and rubber bands, maybe with some added duct tape, all the more power to me for doing so and there are no points lost due to form.

Unfortunately, the Turing Test also has a number of downsides, including that the moderator has to be astute enough to ask suitably probing questions and also be able to ascertain whether the answers reflect whatever we might ascribe as human intelligence.

As something to keep you busy for a while, if you were the moderator, what questions would you ask in the Turing Test setup?

Better come up with some doozies.

Back to the matter at hand, one of the vexing questions about reaching human intelligence is whether there is a need to also achieve sentience.

This brings up another issue, namely what sentience means, just as we earlier had gone through the exercise of trying to figure out what soul means.

Some suggest that sentience is that life-spark that makes us able to reason and think. If so, can an animal be sentient? And, what about a rock? Most would likely say that a rock cannot be sentient, though this is arguable too.

Put on your thinking cap for these tough inquiries:
- If you have sentience, might you also have a soul?
- If you have a soul, must you be ergo sentient?
- Must you have a soul, if you are sentient?
- Are soul and sentience the same, or are they markedly different from each other?

Okay, this takes us to the pinnacle of what this discussion entails.

In order to achieve AI, will the AI need to have a soul?

This also takes us back to those worrisome predictions that Musk and plenty of others have voiced about what AI might regrettably become.

One view is that if we can achieve AI, doing so without imbuing a soul, the result would be a machine that is soulless.

And, if we have a machine that can be as smart as humans (maybe even smarter, the so-called super-intelligence, see my explanation at **this link here**), and yet lacks a soul, will we find ourselves working with a co-equal that doesn't give a wit about having a soul, and therefore might perform dastardly acts that otherwise via the use of a soul they might not have undertaken.

That is why some vehemently have qualms about arriving at AI.

The assumption is that by lacking a soul, and assuming that otherwise, AI can exist (which, as mentioned, we don't know whether a soul is required or not for the AI to achieve human intelligence), the AI is going to be somewhat valueless and act in soulless and undesirable ways.

In addition, maybe the AI would be easily swayed by humans that have despicable deeds in mind. Perhaps the AI would pine away for a soul and be willing to do heinous acts to get one (this is a rather popular theme in sci-fi plots).

For those of you that find this discussion about souls and AI as a bit of a stretch, I certainly understand your discomfort for it.

You might be in the camp that says there is no need for a soul in terms of AI.

In that viewpoint, AI is essentially mechanistic, and you would likely be of a perspective that rocks do not have a soul and therefore neither will AI need to have one. Essentially, a rock and an AI machine are the same, meaning they both are not living creatures and have no business dealing with souls.

Maybe so.

At this juncture, no one can say either way.

There is also a camp that argues that the aspects of "soul" might naturally arise once we get to the point of arriving at AI. In essence, the machine will by some osmosis or other manner just become soulful upon achieving an as-yet-unknown amount of intelligence.

We are woefully far away from that juncture and there's no look-ahead peeking that can yet provide insights on that puzzling conundrum.

Those with a bit of extra boastful bravado in AI would likely insist that if indeed a soul is needed, or even if only desired, this can simply be done via simulation within the AI, and therefore there is no need to fuss about that whole soul-related thing anyway.

One wonders if that might be biting off more than they can chew.

Another added twist takes us back to the soul-selling by Grime.

If humans have a soul, and if humans can impart a part of their soul, could they do so to something other than another human (such as giving a part of their soul to an AI)?

Imagine that.

There is a topper.

If AI ends up having a soul, and if humans can impart a soul to other humans, could an AI impart part of their soul to a human?

Seems like we might find ourselves in quite a pickle of everybody and everyone swapping around souls, perhaps a marketplace or bazaar might spring up, which would not seem to be the prevailing belief about how souls are supposed to be managed and savored.

Self-Driving Cars In This Picture Too

Where do self-driving cars fit in?

Well, we don't know yet whether it will be possible to arrive at a true self-driving car, one that is fully autonomous and able to drive in whatever manner a human can drive, which remains an open question.

There are lots of efforts underway and billions being spent to see if that can be achieved. Even if we cannot get there, perhaps due to not being able to devise sufficiently capable AI, many would argue that the semi-autonomous variants will have demonstrative value in any case.

Some believe that the only way there is to craft true AI, the fully thinking kind, one that would pass a Turing Test.

Time then for some salient questions:
- If only full-fledged AI is required to be able to have true self-driving cars, will that AI have a soul or not?
- If the AI does have a soul, will that alter how it drives a car and how we treat the AI?
- Would the AI be deemed to have human rights?
- How would we know that the AI has a soul?
- Etc.

Conclusion

For those that think the artistry showcase by Grimes is mere puffery, there is another side to that coin, which can get us all to reconsider what we mean by "soul" (an artistic license on her part and having a dual result, one might say).

It is often said that the role of artists is to stir rather lofty and mind-bending questions about our existence, especially so perhaps for those scientists, engineers, and AI developers that are bent on crafting and perfecting their inventions, including AI, all of whom could indubitably use a healthy dose of human-centric thinking as they pursue their revered goals.

Mark this lesson as a venerated window into the soul, for both man and AI.

.

CHAPTER 12
CYBER-HACKERS MAKE MONEY AND AI SELF-DRIVING CARS

CHAPTER 11

CYBER-HACKERS MAKE MONEY

AND

AI SELF-DRIVING CARS

Put those darned cyber-hacker criminals into jail and throw away the key, some exhort daily.

We are all somewhat numbed by the continual announcements about cyber-hackers that have broken into an online database and stolen our personal information, oftentimes doing so via attacking credit reporting agency databases, retailer databases, insurance company databases, financial and banking systems, and the like.

It seems like nearly every day a letter comes in the mail with a notification that your personal identification has been compromised and you are urged to take precautionary measures to be on the watch for someone falsely using your ID and masquerading as you. Those reprehensible uses can harm your credit rating, can smear your reputation, and can hit bluntly your savings or other monies that the hackers might be able to access and deplete.

It is the wild west out there in cyber-land.

Generally, your personal safety is not particularly threatened, though let's be clear that losing the dough in your bank accounts is tantamount to a type of financial menace and livelihood threat that could lead to your becoming destitute or facing other costly repercussions.

As we find ourselves becoming increasingly reliant on computer-controlled physical systems that are within our midst, and as those systems tend to be hooked-up online, the danger of being threatened with actual bodily harm will rise.

One such obvious and frequently cited example is the emergence of AI-based self-driving cars and other similar autonomous vehicles (including self-driving drones, self-driving trucks, and so on).

In short, there is a possibility that a cyber-hacker could intercede in an autonomous vehicle and in one manner or another cause difficulty or worse in terms of impacting the driving aspects of the vehicle.

This concern is one of the most commonly noted qualms when public surveys and polls are taken about the advent of self-driving cars.

For those in the self-driving car industry, there seems to be an ongoing viewpoint by some that though there is a potential minuscule chance of a cyber-hack into a self-driving car, and thus indeed cyber-security is paramount, they nonetheless often state or suggest that there is little incentive for cyber-hackers to target self-driving cars due to the (presumed) lack of money to be made.

In other words, the belief appears to be that since a self-driving car is not a bank, it is not a savings account, it is not a credit card, one must conclude ergo that cyber-hackers will not go out of their way to come after self-driving cars.

To such a perspective, I loudly (and politely) say hogwash, and plead that those promulgating such a stance would reconsider the matter, including that they should forthwith cease and desist in permeating a quite misleading and wholly unsound position.

Let's be above-board, there are plenty of ways for cyber-hackers to make money off of self-driving cars.

In fact, the money-making potential is quite sizable and will indisputably be a crucial factor in why and how cyber-hackers sink their teeth into self-driving cars.

Anyone with a blind spot on this source of motivation will likely underestimate the veracity of the threats that cyber-hackers are going to undertake in this realm.

Maybe this might help: *Follow the money.*

What this means is that if you are already willing to agree that safety is a key aspect of cyber-security and that there is a chance (no matter how slim) that cyber-hackers might seek to undermine the safety of self-driving cars, the money aspects are inextricably intertwined, I assure you.

How so?

I will lay out for you the numerous ways that cyber-hackers have an "opportunity" (dastardly so) to try and make a payday out of self-driving cars.

Before I share those insights, allow me a moment to bring up some related points.

First, whenever I write about cyber-security, there are some that right away complain that by doing so the indications proffered are allowing cyber-hackers to gauge what kinds of cyber protections are being devised and what kinds of cyber vulnerabilities exist.

The worry is that by writing about these topics, it helps the cyber-hackers, arming them accordingly.

Please realize that this is the now-classic head-in-the-sand posturing regarding discussing cyber-security and related matters.

Some believe that we should not talk about, nor write about, and not in any manner even whisper the nature and avenues of cyber-security and cyber-hacking, since it tips a hand to the evildoers.

This is a misguided and ill-informed notion, though one can certainly sympathize with their logic.

Here's the rub.

It is plainly the case that cyber-hackers are going to figure out these same facets, one way or another, and by trying to hide such discussions it does little good, including that it tends to undercut the preparations for and awareness about being on the hunt to stop and prevent cyber-hacking.

A head in the sand translates into getting kicked in the rear, as the old saying goes.

Meanwhile, there is another stated reason to not discuss such matters, namely that by doing so, it will cause mass hysteria.

Again, the logic for this is certainly understandable.

When those writing about cyber-security and cyber-hacking do so irresponsibly, attempting merely to fan the flames of angst, there is no question that such shoddy and perhaps even iniquitous efforts are sad, hurtful, and do not advance sensibly the battle between cyber-security and cyber-hacking.

It is vital that discussions about cyber-crime be taken seriously, somberly, factually, and portray matters in a balanced and rational way.

Okay, so having covered those caveats, let's dive into some background and context of how cyber-security and cyber-hacking come to play related to self-driving cars.

After establishing that foundation, we can then take a close look at how money is an underlying motivator and something not to be ignored, trivialized, or falsely thought as inconsequential.

Speaking of foundations, not everyone knows what it means to refer to a "self-driving car" and so we ought to start there.

The Role of AI-Based Self-Driving Cars

True self-driving cars are ones that the AI drives the car entirely on its own and there isn't any human assistance during the driving task.

These driverless vehicles are considered a Level 4 and Level 5, while a car that requires a human driver to co-share the driving effort is usually considered at a Level 2 or Level 3. The cars that co-share the driving task are described as being semi-autonomous, and typically contain a variety of automated add-on's that are referred to as ADAS (Advanced Driver-Assistance Systems).

There is not yet a true self-driving car at Level 5, which we don't yet even know if this will be possible to achieve, and nor how long it will take to get there.

Meanwhile, the Level 4 efforts are gradually trying to get some traction by undergoing very narrow and selective public roadway trials, though there is controversy over whether this testing should be allowed per se (we are all life-or-death guinea pigs in an experiment taking place on our highways and byways, some point out).

Since semi-autonomous cars require a human driver, the adoption of those types of cars won't be markedly different than driving conventional vehicles, so there's not much new per se to cover about them on this topic (though, as you'll see in a moment, the points next made are generally applicable).

For semi-autonomous cars, it is important that the public needs to be forewarned about a disturbing aspect that's been arising lately, namely that in spite of those human drivers that keep posting videos of themselves falling asleep at the wheel of a Level 2 or Level 3 car, we all need to avoid being misled into believing that the driver can take away their attention from the driving task while driving a semi-autonomous car.

You are the responsible party for the driving actions of the vehicle, regardless of how much automation might be tossed into a Level 2 or Level 3.

Self-Driving Cars And Hacking Levels

For Level 4 and Level 5 true self-driving vehicles, there won't be a human driver involved in the driving task.

All occupants will be passengers.

The AI is doing the driving.

Generally, most automakers are anticipating removing entirely the human-accessible driving controls from Level 4 and Level 5 self-driving cars. They do not have to do so per se since there is not a requirement across-the-board to do so, but it makes sense that they would likely want to do this.

Why so?

Simply stated, if you believe that human drivers have driving foibles, which we know they do, and we know that for example there are right now about 40,000 annual deaths due to car crashes in the United States alone, along with approximately 2.3 million injuries, it seems prudent to take away the driving from humans.

And, if the AI can do the driving, doing so without any need for a human driver, settle the matter by denying driving access for the human occupants.

Before pursuing that aspect in the context of cyber-hacking and cyber-security, consider the Level 2 and Level 3 cars.

As mentioned, those are cars that involve the co-sharing of the driving task.

Keep in mind then the Level 4 and Level 5 will generally be minus driving controls for humans, while the Level 2 and Level 3 will have such controls and yet also involve the co-sharing of the driving with the automation of the car.

Some would say that the downside of the Level 4 and Level 5 is that if a cyber-hacker were to take over the driving controls, which at this point in the discussion I'm not saying is likely or not likely, but we ought to agree that there is a chance of it, which we might debate about the probability, but it is an existent chance, the human occupants have no ready or apparent means to try and overtake the overtaking of the driving controls.

That's what causes some people to especially shudder about self-driving cars and the risks associated with a cyber-hack.

For them, they sometimes believe that with a Level 2 or Level 3, the human driver either will not suffer at the hands of a cyber-hack or that if they do, since the human driver is at the wheel, they will simply overtake the overtaking.

I would not be so sanguine about Level 2 and Level 3.

If the steering suddenly and unexpectedly makes a wild veer to the right, and the car is going say 65 miles per hour, and there is a wall there, it seems mighty doubtful that the human driver is going to realize what is happening and even if they do it will likely be too late to react.

The point being that cyber-hacks can wreak havoc on not just Level 4 and Level 5, which is usually where all the attention and anguish seems to go but can just as likely impact the Level 2 and Level 3 cars, and that a human sitting in the driver's seat does not especially bolster the chances of averting the hack (of course, it depends on what kind of hack is occurring).

Some will begrudgingly concur about the Level 2 and Level 3 qualms, but they would argue that the humans riding in a self-driving car are essentially sitting ducks, not having any direct and immediate means to overcome a hack, while the human driver in the less-so automated cars has at least a chance of taking action.

I would counterargue that you are discussing a sentiment allegorically akin to the moving of deckchairs around on the deck of the Titanic, namely that the human driver in a Level 2 or Level 3 is not likely to make a substantive difference when a significant hack occurs.

Couple that notion with the fact that human drivers can potentially exacerbate the matter.

Allow me to explain.

Suppose a cyber-hack causes a Level 2 or Level 3 car to slightly veer off-course, but the human driver freaks out and way over-controls, possibly leading the vehicle into doom which otherwise might not have arisen.

Or, suppose that human drivers are aware of the chances of cyber-hacks, so they sit on the edge, waiting for the day that it might happen, and end-up at times radically over-controlling their car, even though let's say that no cyber-hack has been activated (it is a ghost implanted in their minds).

There are about 250 million licensed drivers in the United States today, and one blanches at the notion that those humans still driving cars will be on pins-and-needles, leading to some percentage of newly classified car crashes as ones that were prompted due to the human driver believing their car was under cyber-attack.

It could be a huge multiplier effect when applied across hundreds of millions of human drivers.

In recap, cyber-hacking will impact not just Level 4 and Level 5, but Level 2 and Level 3 too, and the cars that allow human driving will not be immune to hacks and nor does the presence of a human driver afford necessarily a heightened measure of safety thereof (including that it could be potentially less safe).

Show Me The Money

I trust that you are now open-minded that there are cyber-hacks that could impact Level 2, Level 3, Level 4, and Level 5 cars, and thus we can judiciously consider that there is vulnerability to go all around, no matter the level of the vehicle (other than ones that have essentially no automation, or that have no connectivity allowing for cyber-hacking, though they could still be hacked possibly one at a time via the use of the OBD-II, see my discussion at **this link here**).

From a safety perspective, I assume too that we can all agree that if a cyber-hack is devious enough and able enough, it could cause a vehicle to ram into a wall, or strike pedestrians, or smash into other nearby cars.

Again, put aside for a moment the chances of those acts, since I realize that some will jump up and instantly claim that the odds of those occurring are slim. My focus is that they could happen and as such, what else does that comport.

Time for the money.

We'll start with the simplest variant.

Cyber-hackers are sometimes motivated by the notoriety that can be had via a highly visible and bone-chilling hack. Besides the self-aggrandizement, some of those cyber-hackers parlay their gained reputation into other acts.

In short, if one could hack a self-driving car, it could bolster their street cred, which in turn might bring them monetary offers of doing the same or other kinds of cyber-hacking, leading to a payday.

Essentially, they hire themselves out as a "proven" cyber-hacker, acting as a paid mercenary for other heinous cyber-hacking efforts. You won't though be able to attract much dough if you do not have a calling card, as it were, and the potential of enormous publicity from a self-driving car hack is a whopper of a boost.

You might be carping that this seems somewhat indirect, but nonetheless, it is a bona fide and real-world possibility of tying this kind of cyber-hacking to money.

Shift gears and consider the more direct routes to money.

I have one word for you: *Ransomware.*

Imagine a cyber-hacker that has concocted some nefarious exploit for a particular brand of a self-driving car.

They perhaps employ it on one or two such vehicles, showcasing what they can get away with. Then, they contact the fleet owner of the self-driving cars and/or the automakers, and undertake a ransom threat, seeking money to either undo the exploit or reveal how the exploit works, etc.

What will the fleet owners and automakers do?

Some of you might be bellowing that no fleet owner and no automaker would ever pay such a ransom.

If you are making such a declaration, you might want to look more closely at the massive size of the ransomware marketplace.

You might also want to contemplate the aspects of a nation-state that might be (reluctantly or overtly) willing to pay such a ransom.

Consider another example of a money-making path, similar to the ransomware route.

A cyber-hacker with a self-driving car self-made exploit might decide to post the existence of the exploit as available for auction, seeking the highest bidder that might want to purchase it.

In this use case, the cyber-hacker is likely thinking that it is too risky to try and use the exploit themselves, so why not instead sell the thing and pocket the dough, secretly, without as much exposure, and then presumably start on their next sellable exploit.

Likely, for "proof" that the exploit is real and demonstrative, the cyber-hacker might use it on a vehicle and perhaps videotape the result or otherwise offer evidence to showcase that the exploit is not vaporware.

Overall, I believe you get the gist, which is that money ties to safety (hacking), and safety (hacking) ties to money.

Rest assured that there is a slew of additional ways to make money by cyber-hacking self-driving cars (that is a glum thought).

I won't go into them all here.

There is a twist though that is worthwhile to consider.

Conclusion

The twist is that we are lamentably going to be confronted with scammers on these matters.

Here's how that will work.

A scammer that does not have any kind of exploit will pretend that they do have something in hand.

In that case, repeat all the points I made about the cyber-hackers that do have actual hacks, except the scammer does not, but manages to fool people into believing that they do.

This will not only impact the fleet owners and automakers, but such scams are going to open the door to scamming everyday people.

For those people that right now respond by sending money when they believe that a Nigerian royal member has left them a fortune, you can add the self-driving car cyber-hack scams.

Consider this stomach-wrenching use case. A despicable scammer contacts someone, tells them that there is a hack associated with self-driving cars that can be operated remotely and that whichever self-driving car the person uses for ride-sharing or whatever purpose, the exploit is ready to be used. If the person will transfer funds or give up their credit card or pay some bitcoins, they will never be harmed by any such exploit, so the scammer assures.

Scammers will always exist and find new ways to scam, including in the case of self-driving cars, woefully so.

Not wanting to end this discussion on such a sour note, since we know that these are possibilities, along with the inarguable allure of money, we can attempt to mitigate these evildoers by bolstering cyber-security and by engaging the public in awareness on these matters, responsibly.

And, as perhaps a silver lining, maybe we can get the bad-hat hackers to switch over to the good-hat side of hacking, offering them the altruistic notion of helping mankind and simultaneously making money by finding exploits that they then get a bounty for discovering, or by enlisting them in the protection of self-driving cars for a steady paycheck and a bountiful peace of mind.

That seems to be the way that the wild west was won.

APPENDIX

Dr. Lance B. Eliot

APPENDIX A
TEACHING WITH THIS MATERIAL

The material in this book can be readily used either as a supplemental to other content for a class, or it can also be used as a core set of textbook material for a specialized class. Classes where this material is most likely used include any classes at the college or university level that want to augment the class by offering thought provoking and educational essays about AI and self-driving cars.

In particular, here are some aspects for class use:

o <u>Computer Science</u>. Studying AI, autonomous vehicles, etc.

o <u>Business</u>. Exploring technology and it adoption for business.

o <u>Sociology</u>. Sociological views on the adoption and advancement of technology.

Specialized classes at the undergraduate and graduate level can also make use of this material.

For each chapter, consider whether you think the chapter provides material relevant to your course topic. There is plenty of opportunity to get the students thinking about the topic and force them to decide whether they agree or disagree with the points offered and positions taken. I would also encourage you to have the students do additional research beyond the chapter material presented (I provide next some suggested assignments they can do).

RESEARCH ASSIGNMENTS ON THESE TOPICS

Your students can find background material on these topics, doing so in various business and technical publications. I list below the top ranked AI related journals. For business publications, I would suggest the usual culprits such as the Harvard Business Review, Forbes, Fortune, WSJ, and the like.

Here are some suggestions of homework or projects that you could assign to students:

a) Assignment for foundational AI research topic: Research and prepare a paper and a presentation on a specific aspect of Deep AI, Machine Learning, ANN, etc. The paper should cite at least 3 reputable sources. Compare and contrast to what has been stated in this book.

b) Assignment for the Self-Driving Car topic: Research and prepare a paper and Self-Driving Cars. Cite at least 3 reputable sources and analyze the characterizations. Compare and contrast to what has been stated in this book.

c) Assignment for a Business topic: Research and prepare a paper and a presentation on businesses and advanced technology. What is hot, and what is not? Cite at least 3 reputable sources. Compare and contrast to the depictions in this book.

d) Assignment to do a Startup: Have the students prepare a paper about how they might startup a business in this realm. They must submit a sound Business Plan for the startup. They could also be asked to present their Business Plan and so should also have a presentation deck to coincide with it.

You can certainly adjust the aforementioned assignments to fit to your particular needs and the class structure. You'll notice that I ask for 3 reputable cited sources for the paper writing based assignments. I usually steer students toward "reputable" publications, since otherwise they will cite some oddball source that has no credentials other than that they happened to write something and post it onto the Internet. You can define "reputable" in whatever way you prefer, for example some faculty think Wikipedia is not reputable while others believe it is reputable and allow students to cite it.

The reason that I usually ask for at least 3 citations is that if the student only does one or two citations they usually settle on whatever they happened to find the fastest. By requiring three citations, it usually seems to force them to look around, explore, and end-up probably finding five or more, and then whittling it down to 3 that they will actually use.

I have not specified the length of their papers, and leave that to you to tell the students what you prefer. For each of those assignments, you could end-up with a short one to two pager, or you could do a dissertation length paper. Base the length on whatever best fits for your class, and the credit amount of the assignment within the context of the other grading metrics you'll be using for the class.

I mention in the assignments that they are to do a paper and prepare a presentation. I usually try to get students to present their work. This is a good practice for what they will do in the business world. Most of the time, they will be required to prepare an analysis and present it. If you don't have the class time or inclination to have the students present, then you can of course cut out the aspect of them putting together a presentation.

If you want to point students toward highly ranked journals in AI, here's a list of the top journals as reported by *various citation counts sources* (this list changes year to year):

o   Communications of the ACM

o   Artificial Intelligence

o   Cognitive Science

o   IEEE Transactions on Pattern Analysis and Machine Intelligence

o   Foundations and Trends in Machine Learning

o   Journal of Memory and Language

o   Cognitive Psychology

o   Neural Networks

o   IEEE Transactions on Neural Networks and Learning Systems

o   IEEE Intelligent Systems

o   Knowledge-based Systems

GUIDE TO USING THE CHAPTERS

For each of the chapters, I provide next some various ways to use the chapter material. You can assign the tasks as individual homework assignments, or the tasks can be used with team projects for the class. You can easily layout a series of assignments, such as indicating that the students are to do item "a" below for say Chapter 1, then "b" for the next chapter of the book, and so on.

a) What is the main point of the chapter and describe in your own words the significance of the topic,

b) Identify at least two aspects in the chapter that you agree with, and support your concurrence by providing at least one other outside researched item as support; make sure to explain your basis for disagreeing with the aspects,

c) Identify at least two aspects in the chapter that you disagree with, and support your disagreement by providing at least one other outside researched item as support; make sure to explain your basis for disagreeing with the aspects,

d) Find an aspect that was not covered in the chapter, doing so by conducting outside research, and then explain how that aspect ties into the chapter and what significance it brings to the topic,

e) Interview a specialist in industry about the topic of the chapter, collect from them their thoughts and opinions, and readdress the chapter by citing your source and how they compared and contrasted to the material,

f) Interview a relevant academic professor or researcher in a college or university about the topic of the chapter, collect from them their thoughts and opinions, and readdress the chapter by citing your source and how they compared and contrasted to the material,

g) Try to update a chapter by finding out the latest on the topic, and ascertain whether the issue or topic has now been solved or whether it is still being addressed, explain what you come up with.

The above are all ways in which you can get the students of your class involved in considering the material of a given chapter. You could mix things up by having one of those above assignments per each week, covering the chapters over the course of the semester or quarter.

As a reminder, here are the chapters of the book and you can select whichever chapters you find most valued for your particular class:

Chapter Title

1 Eliot Framework for AI Self-Driving Cars

2 AI Oligopolies and AI Self-Driving Cars

3 AI Intent and AI Self-Driving Cars

4 "Life On Wheels" Film and AI Self-Driving Cars

5 Murder Hornet Spread and AI Self-Driving Cars

6 Simons Sight Research and AI Self-Driving Cars

7 NASCAR Car Racing and AI Self-Driving Cars

8 Ballot Harvesting and AI Self-Driving Cars

9 Apollo 12 Lessons and AI Self-Driving Cars

10 Running Over Shooter and AI Self-Driving Cars

11 Grimes Soul Selling and AI Self-Driving Cars

12 Cyber-Hackers Make Money and AI Self-Driving Cars

Companion Book By This Author

Advances in AI and Autonomous Vehicles: Cybernetic Self-Driving Cars

Practical Advances in Artificial Intelligence (AI) and Machine Learning

by

Dr. Lance B. Eliot, MBA, PhD

This title is available via Amazon and other book sellers

This title is available via Amazon and other book seller

This title is available via Amazon and other book sellers

This title is available via Amazon and other book sellers

Companion Book By This Author

Introduction to
Driverless Self-Driving Cars

by Dr. Lance B. Eliot, MBA, PhD

This title is available via Amazon and other book sellers

This title is available via Amazon and other book sellers

Companion Book By This Author

Transformative Artificial Intelligence Driverless Self-Driving Cars

by Dr. Lance B. Eliot, MBA, PhD

This title is available via Amazon and other book sellers

Companion Book By This Author

Disruptive Artificial Intelligence and Driverless Self-Driving Cars

by Dr. Lance B. Eliot, MBA, PhD

This title is available via Amazon and other book sellers

Companion Book By This Author

State-of-the-Art
AI Driverless Self-Driving Cars
by Dr. Lance B. Eliot, MBA, PhD

This title is available via Amazon and other book sellers

This title is available via Amazon and other book sellers

Companion Book By This Author

AI Innovations and Self-Driving Cars

by Dr. Lance B. Eliot, MBA, PhD

This title is available via Amazon and other book sellers

Companion Book By This Author

Crucial Advances for
AI Self-Driving Cars

by Dr. Lance B. Eliot, MBA, PhD

This title is available via Amazon and other book sellers

Companion Book By This Author

Sociotechnical Insights and AI Driverless Cars

by Dr. Lance B. Eliot, MBA, PhD

<u>Chapter Title</u>

This title is available via Amazon and other book sellers

Companion Book By This Author

Pioneering Advances for AI Driverless Cars

by Dr. Lance B. Eliot, MBA, PhD

Chapter Title

1   Eliot Framework for AI Self-Driving Cars

2   Boxes on Wheels and AI Self-Driving Cars

3   Clogs and AI Self-Driving Cars

4   Kids Communicating with AI Self-Driving Cars

5   Incident Awareness and AI Self-Driving Car

6   Emotion Recognition and Self-Driving Cars

7   Rear-End Collisions and AI Self-Driving Cars

8   Autonomous Nervous System and AI Self-Driving Cars

9   Height Warnings and AI Self-Driving Cars

10 Future Jobs and AI Self-Driving Cars

11 Car Wash and AI Self-Driving Cars

12 5G and AI Self-Driving Cars

13 Gen Z and AI Self-Driving Cars

This title is available via Amazon and other book sellers

Companion Book By This Author

Leading Edge Trends for AI Driverless Cars

by Dr. Lance B. Eliot, MBA, PhD

This title is available via Amazon and other book sellers

This title is available via Amazon and other book sellers

Companion Book By This Author

***The Next Wave of
AI Self-Driving Cars***

by Dr. Lance B. Eliot, MBA, PhD

<u>Chapter Title</u>

1 Eliot Framework for AI Self-Driving Cars

2 Productivity and AI Self-Driving Cars

3 Blind Pedestrians and AI Self-Driving Cars

4 Fail-Safe AI and AI Self-Driving Cars

5 Anomaly Detection and AI Self-Driving Cars

6 Running Out of Gas and AI Self-Driving Cars

7 Deep Personalization and AI Self-Driving Cars

8 Reframing the Levels of AI Self-Driving Cars

9 Cryptojacking and AI Self-Driving Cars

This title is available via Amazon and other book sellers

Companion Book By This Author

Revolutionary Innovations of AI Self-Driving Cars

by Dr. Lance B. Eliot, MBA, PhD

Chapter Title

This title is available via Amazon and other book sellers

Companion Book By This Author

AI Self-Driving Cars
Breakthroughs

by Dr. Lance B. Eliot, MBA, PhD

Chapter Title

This title is available via Amazon and other book sellers

Companion Book By This Author

***Trailblazing Trends* for
AI Self-Driving Cars**

by Dr. Lance B. Eliot, MBA, PhD

Chapter Title

This title is available via Amazon and other book sellers

Companion Book By This Author

***Ingenious Strides for*
AI Driverless Cars**

by Dr. Lance B. Eliot, MBA, PhD

Chapter Title

1 Eliot Framework for AI Self-Driving Cars

2 Plasticity and AI Self-Driving Cars

3 NIMBY vs. YIMBY and AI Self-Driving Cars

4 Top Trends for 2019 and AI Self-Driving Cars

5 Rural Areas and AI Self-Driving Cars

6 Self-Imposed Constraints and AI Self-Driving Car

7 Alien Limb Syndrome and AI Self-Driving Cars

8 Jaywalking and AI Self-Driving Cars

This title is available via Amazon and other book sellers

<u>Companion Book By This Author</u>

AI Self-Driving Cars
Inventiveness

by Dr. Lance B. Eliot, MBA, PhD

<u>Chapter Title</u>

This title is available via Amazon and other book sellers

Companion Book By This Author

Visionary Secrets of
AI Driverless Cars

by Dr. Lance B. Eliot, MBA, PhD

This title is available via Amazon and other book sellers

Companion Book By This Author

Spearheading
AI Self-Driving Cars

by Dr. Lance B. Eliot, MBA, PhD

This title is available via Amazon and other book sellers

Companion Book By This Author

Spurring
AI Self-Driving Cars
by Dr. Lance B. Eliot, MBA, PhD

This title is available via Amazon and other book sellers

Companion Book By This Author

Avant-Garde
AI Driverless Cars

by Dr. Lance B. Eliot, MBA, PhD

Chapter Title

This title is available via Amazon and other book sellers

Companion Book By This Author

AI Self-Driving Cars
Evolvement

by Dr. Lance B. Eliot, MBA, PhD

This title is available via Amazon and other book sellers

<u>Companion Book By This Author</u>

AI Driverless Cars
Chrysalis

by Dr. Lance B. Eliot, MBA, PhD

<u>Chapter Title</u>

This title is available via Amazon and other book sellers

Companion Book By This Author

Boosting
AI Autonomous Cars
by Dr. Lance B. Eliot, MBA, PhD

This title is available via Amazon and other book sellers

<u>Companion Book By This Author</u>

AI Self-Driving Cars
Trendsetting

by Dr. Lance B. Eliot, MBA, PhD

<u>Chapter Title</u>

This title is available via Amazon and other book sellers

Companion Book By This Author

AI Autonomous Cars Forefront

by Dr. Lance B. Eliot, MBA, PhD

This title is available via Amazon and other book sellers

Companion Book By This Author

AI Autonomous Cars Emergence

by Dr. Lance B. Eliot, MBA, PhD

This title is available via Amazon and other book sellers

<u>Companion Book By This Author</u>

AI Autonomous Cars Progress

by Dr. Lance B. Eliot, MBA, PhD

<u>Chapter Title</u>

This title is available via Amazon and other book sellers

Companion Book By This Author

AI Self-Driving Cars
Prognosis

by Dr. Lance B. Eliot, MBA, PhD

This title is available via Amazon and other book sellers

Companion Book By This Author

AI Self-Driving Cars
Momentum

by Dr. Lance B. Eliot, MBA, PhD

This title is available via Amazon and other book sellers

Companion Book By This Author

AI Self-Driving Cars
Headway
by Dr. Lance B. Eliot, MBA, PhD

Chapter Title

1 Eliot Framework for AI Self-Driving Cars

2 Germs Spreading and AI Self-Driving Cars

3 Carbon Footprint and AI Self-Driving Cars

4 Protestors Use Of AI Self-Driving Cars

5 Rogue Behavior and AI Self-Driving Cars

6 Using Human Drivers Versus AI Self-Driving Cars

7 Tesla Hodge-Podge On AI Self-Driving Cars

8 Solo Occupancy and AI Self-Driving Cars

9 Einstein's Twins Paradox and AI Self-Driving Cars

10 Nation-State Takeover Of AI Self-Driving Cars

11 Quantum Computers and AI Self-Driving Cars

12 Religious Revival And AI Self-Driving Cars

This title is available via Amazon and other book sellers

Companion Book By This Author

AI Self-Driving Cars
Vicissitude

by Dr. Lance B. Eliot, MBA, PhD

This title is available via Amazon and other book sellers

<u>Companion Book By This Author</u>

AI Self-Driving Cars
Autonomy

by Dr. Lance B. Eliot, MBA, PhD

This title is available via Amazon and other book sellers

Companion Book By This Author

AI Driverless Cars Transmutation

by Dr. Lance B. Eliot, MBA, PhD

This title is available via Amazon and other book sellers

Companion Book By This Author

***AI Driverless Cars
Potentiality***

by Dr. Lance B. Eliot, MBA, PhD

Chapter Title

1   Eliot Framework for AI Self-Driving Cars

2   Russian Values and AI Self-Driving Cars

3   Friendships Uplift and AI Self-Driving Cars

4   Dogs Driving and AI Self-Driving Cars

5   Hypodermic Needles and AI Self-Driving Cars

6   Sharing Self-Driving Tech Is Not Likely

7   Uber Driver "Kidnapper" Is Self-Driving Car Lesson

8   Gender Driving Biases In AI Self-Driving Cars

9   Slain Befriended Dolphins Are Self-Driving Car Lesson

10   Analysis Of AI In Government Report

11   Mobility Frenzy and AI Self-Driving Cars

This title is available via Amazon and other book sellers

Companion Book By This Author

AI Driverless Cars
Realities

by Dr. Lance B. Eliot, MBA, PhD

Chapter Title

This title is available via Amazon and other book sellers

Companion Book By This Author

AI Self-Driving Cars
Materiality

by Dr. Lance B. Eliot, MBA, PhD

This title is available via Amazon and other book sellers

Companion Book By This Author

AI Self-Driving Cars
Accordance

by Dr. Lance B. Eliot, MBA, PhD

This title is available via Amazon and other book sellers

Companion Book By This Author

AI Self-Driving Cars
Equanimity
by Dr. Lance B. Eliot, MBA, PhD

Chapter Title

This title is available via Amazon and other book sellers

ABOUT THE AUTHOR

Dr. Lance B. Eliot, Ph.D., MBA is a globally recognized AI expert and thought leader, an experienced executive and leader, a successful serial entrepreneur, and a noted scholar on AI, including that his Forbes and AI Trends columns have amassed over 2.8+ million views, his books on AI are frequently ranked in the Top 10 of all-time AI books, his journal articles are widely cited, and he has developed and fielded dozens of AI systems.

He currently serves as the CEO of Techbruim, Inc. and has over twenty years of industry experience including serving as a corporate officer in billion-dollar sized firms and was a partner in a major consulting firm. He is also a successful entrepreneur having founded, ran, and sold several high-tech related businesses.

Dr. Eliot previously hosted the popular radio show *Technotrends* that was also available on American Airlines flights via their in-flight audio program, he has made appearances on CNN, has been a frequent speaker at industry conferences, and his podcasts have been downloaded over 100,000 times.

A former professor at the University of Southern California (USC), he founded and led an innovative research lab on Artificial Intelligence. He also previously served on the faculty of the University of California Los Angeles (UCLA) and was a visiting professor at other major universities. He was elected to the International Board of the Society for Information Management (SIM), a prestigious association of over 3,000 high-tech executives worldwide.

He has performed extensive community service, including serving as Senior Science Adviser to the Congressional Vice-Chair of the Congressional Committee on Science & Technology. He has served on the Board of the OC Science & Engineering Fair (OCSEF), where he is also has been a Grand Sweepstakes judge, and likewise served as a judge for the Intel International SEF (ISEF). He served as the Vice-Chair of the Association for Computing Machinery (ACM) Chapter, a prestigious association of computer scientists. Dr. Eliot has been a shark tank judge for the USC Mark Stevens Center for Innovation on start-up pitch competitions and served as a mentor for several incubators and accelerators in Silicon Valley and in Silicon Beach.

Dr. Eliot holds a Ph.D. from USC, MBA, and Bachelor's in Computer Science, and earned the CDP, CCP, CSP, CDE, and CISA certifications.

ADDENDUM

AI Self-Driving Cars
Equanimity

Practical Advances in Artificial Intelligence (AI)
and Machine Learning

By
Dr. Lance B. Eliot, MBA, PhD

———

For supplemental materials of this book, visit:
www.ai-selfdriving-cars.guru

For special orders of this book, contact:
LBE Press Publishing
Email: LBE.Press.Publishing@gmail.com